Mumma,
Can You Hear Me?

Mumma, Can You Hear Me?

Copyright © 2012 by Betty Williams. All US and international rights reserved.

This is a work of nonfiction. Great care has been taken to portray people, entities, and events as accurately and fairly as possible. Some names may have been changed to protect persons living or deceased.

We founded f/64 Publishing to promote crisp, clear storytelling that captures those details essential to understanding a subject. Like making a photographic exposure at f/64, this takes time and strategy...and can result in breathtaking work. The company is also named partly in honor of the association of photographers co-founded by Ansel Adams: Group f.64.

f/64 Publishing
60 Wellwood Rd | Portland, ME 04103 USA
www.f64publishing.com
www.MummaCanYouHearMe.com

Cover Design © 2012 Elizabeth Zanter. Used by permission.
Interior Design © 2012 Dave Norman. All rights reserved.
Editorial support by Karen White.
Poem "I Am Strong, You Know," © 1977 James Kavanaugh

1. Biography & Autobiography : Personal Memoirs
2. Religion : Christian Life - General
3. Biography & Autobiography : General

ISBN 13: 978-0-9831858-3-3
Written and published in the USA

For Those Who
Have Loved Me

Also available from f/64 Publishing

Leading Jake

Following Josh

White River Junctions

A Small Town Celebration

Contents

Appendices

Mumma

God gave her heavenly wisdom and insight
Way beyond her knowledge
She knew when to coddle, discipline, or laugh
Things not learned in college
She somehow knew when to hold on,
But also when to let go
She gave love and acceptance, filled with
Encouragement to grow

Her life was full of living and
She filled the lives of others
When God chose her for me, He gave
The Nobel Prize of mothers

My Mother? She is an angel smiling down on me
She is a gentle breeze of hope,
Pushing me strongly ahead
She is the laughter of my blue-eyed grandson
Reaching out to me
She is a salty tear on my cheek and lips
When sorrow touches me
She is the pure waxy petal of a gardenia
Filling my life with a lovely fragrance
My Mother

- **Betty Williams**

Chapter I

Life Goes On

*A*lthough the grassy mound I was sitting on was dry and warm, the day was strangely gray and quiet. Here in the cemetery, it was as though my mother and I were a million miles away from the rest of the world. My head was full of questions—ones that I had never asked, with the answers hidden now in the past. "Mumma, who were you?" I ask the stillness. "How did you manage to care for seven children when you were all alone in this world? How did you spend so little time with me and still make me feel so understood, cared for, and loved? How did you, with so little schooling, instill in me a love for Henry Wadsworth Longfellow, Shakespeare, and the Bible?

"Mumma, why couldn't you have lived long enough to help guide me through the rest of my life? I had God, but oh how I needed you..."

* * * * *

When her divorce was final she found herself alone with five small children from two to twelve to support with no outside help—it was no wonder she felt that the only way to provide for us was to place the oldest and youngest boys with friends and the three of us girls in a children's home while she found work and a place where we could all live together. The beautiful home my father built no longer welcomed us, and neither were we welcome at our grandfather's house directly across the street. We were disowned by our father and grandfather, but always loved by God...and Mumma. The pain she must have felt from being separated from all she had known and loved must have been so great.

My attitude did not help matters. I kicked, screamed, and yelled when brought to the children's home. "I'm not staying here," I bellowed, "and you can't make me!" Did I really think that as a little squirt of four years that I could back up my words? Then, an Ugly Stranger came into the room, asking me if perhaps there was something I had always wanted—sort of like the falsely kind witch in Hansel and Gretel. I immediately thought of a pink bed I had coveted for so long. Maybe this was one of those once in a lifetime situations where I could bow out gracefully from a losing situation, gaining something in the process, and maybe I should go for it. The Ugly Stranger readily agreed to such a simple compromise—a pink bed for my compliance—and in the depths of my heart, I never forgave her for not keeping her promise. After all, how much could a small can of pink paint cost?

Actually, placing me in that children's home was God's way of molding my life, making my heart tender towards children; but I didn't know that then. All through the years I have complained loudly to God about things I did not agree with. Later in life, when my youngest daughter was taken from me to fight the war in Iraq, my screams must have had the angels in Heaven putting their hands over their ears. I fought so hard against it, shutting myself off from people around me so as to better confront God. Deep inside me, I heard that Quiet Voice tell me, "I need to mold and shape this young lady into the person that can be best used on Earth."

My response was, "No problem, Lord; but please do it another way! All means are at Your disposal, and it is within Your power to keep her here and still bring about these things." Imagine me, trying to tell God how to run lives! God did not change His plans. Instead, He gave me the grace to accept them.

Even my loudest objections to being left in a children's home did no good either. God's ways are just not our ways.

* * * * *

In the children's home, I didn't truly live; I merely existed for three long years. The highlight of my life was when Mumma came on Saturdays to visit and to bring laughter and love into our dreary, loveless lives. I hated the oatmeal gruel we were fed for breakfast every morning and would gladly have given my portion to Oliver Twist. My punishment for refusing to eat it was being sent to bed right after supper. With no television, radio, or books, I soon developed the skill of making up stories in my head. To this day I do not know if this is a freak thing or a common thing; perhaps it was just a survival skill for me.

Once a month, the Ugly Stranger tossed pennies out of an upstairs window, and we were all allowed to pick up one to spend on Mary Janes or Squirrel Nut Zippers candy. Later in life, I was told that throwing money at us was a very humiliating thing to do to children, but I loved it. I have never been a very proud person, and all my life I have had to scramble for pennies in one way or another.

Although we were three sisters, and all in the children's home together, I do not remember sister Jean being around much. Being five years older than I, she was put in another dorm. Little did we realize that it would be four years of living under the strong arm of the Ugly Stranger, during which time we would not see our two brothers! Jibby was only two when we left, so he was not really missed; in fact, quite the opposite. Dooley, at fourteen, was probably preoccupied in trying to help you, Mumma, since he had suddenly become the man of the family. Mary and I were in the same dorm, and I remember how unhappy she was.

One day I was quietly sitting on a tire swing and overheard two girls talking and planning to run away. I recognized Mary's voice, declaring how she could easily find her way home. While pacing around, they discovered me close by and threatened my life if I tattled on them. The pair took off that night. The next morning brought sheer confusion, but nothing the Ugly Stranger threatened me with could make me snitch. Not one child was allowed to get out of bed while we were questioned over and over.

Police invaded our dorm, but gained no information. Some kids were getting hungry, but not I. Withholding breakfast was not a problem; I was not going to eat their nasty porridge anyway. Then excitement was in the air when the police brought the two girls back. When I learned they had gone directly to an aunt's house, I felt they should have hidden for awhile first, making the police really work. Were you told that Mary had run away, Mumma, or was this incident kept a secret? They didn't share everything with you.

I remember a childless old couple that wanted to adopt me. The home allowed them to take me for a few days. They bought me a pink, ruffled Shirley Temple dress and had a studio do a portrait of me. The light made my jet-black Dutch-cut hair look as though I had a blue halo on my head. Ha! I remember how angry you were when I told you about this one day. There was some fine print in the papers you signed when placing us there that said if you missed two consecutive visits, an adoption could legally happen. With no car, how did you manage those seven-mile trips? Did you walk?

I guess seven miles is nothing for a mother's conquering love.

* * * * *

I was very small for a four-year-old girl, and felt all alone in a crowd. Sometimes I dreamed vivid nightmares. Once I awoke in the middle of the night to see a little man squatting boldly in the corner made by the open door pressing against my bed. He looked like a bald-headed little Indian. After covering my head for awhile and then taking another look, I saw him still there, grinning at me. After letting out a blood-curdling scream, I jumped out of bed and ran one way as he went the other. The last I saw of him was his quick departure out the floor-length window that led to the fire escape.

I ran to Mattie, the housekeeper, and climbed into her bed, shivering and sobbing. She let me stay there, trying to console me and explaining that it was just a really bad dream. Years later, I went back to visit the children's home and the second-story dormitory where I had slept. The window, fire escape, and door were still there, but no Indian. I did, however, learn that mine was no nightmare—an escapee from a mental institution really had been there!

Even though a child, I could have handled the situation much better had I been told the truth. Adults tend to underestimate children. The part that frightened me most was the fear that I could have a dream that seemed so real; they let me believe this for their sake.

How the brain picks and chooses which childhood memories to lock in is a mystery.

I remember walking alone to Park Hill School from the children's home to attend kindergarten. The worst part was walking past the fire chief's beautiful house where his vicious dog would come out and chase me halfway down the block. It took all the willpower I could muster not to wet my pants before reaching my destination, but sometimes I could not muster enough. My teacher would greet me with, "Run, Betty, run!" It seems to me that down through the years I have heard these same words repeated often—"Run, Betty, run!"—intimating that some disaster could take place if I didn't run fast enough. Even back then, Mumma, God was preparing me and teaching me how to overcome adversities.

From my first day of school I have always had a knack for frustrating teachers—sometimes deliberately, sometimes not. Phonics was unheard of, so we were made to memorize whole words and know them by sight. The teacher would hold up a word, read it, and tell us to remember it. I worked hard to remember each new set of words, hoping to please her, so she would not have to repeat herself. When she held cards up for the second time, I was first to read them. I was so proud...but it was a fine reward I had—she booted me out of my lovely class into the next grade up. I had worked hard to make friends where I was, but now I would have to start all over.

Years later, I hated high school and tried to quit a few times. On one such occasion, the principal called me into his office. He looked quite stern sitting there but finally cleared his throat and declared, "I have been going over your schedule and can find nothing different on Wednesday than any other day, and yet you are absent every Wednesday. Why?"

"Oh," I quickly replied. "That's easy. I can only take two days at a time. So, I rest on Wednesdays." He never approached me again on that subject. Actually, I had quit school a few weeks earlier! And it was two weeks before you discovered it, Mumma. What you said to me burned a spot in my heart and was never forgotten. You told me, "I have never been really demanding or required too much of you, but now I am asking you to please go back and do what it takes to finish high school. I never had this opportunity and want it so much for you." Needless to say, I did it for you—or so I thought.

* * * * *

But back to elementary school... There was dear little Annabelle in my new first grade class. She had beautiful clothes, shiny golden curls, and a complexion like peaches and cream. One day our whole class was allowed to go outside, and Annabelle, dressed in pink tights, tutu, and ballet slippers, gracefully glided up and down the school steps; she was a fantasy come to life, and also my introduction to what life could be like for a child beyond the walls of a children's home.

My mind jumps ahead to other memories of school experiences as I realize how important early impressions are. Teachers play such important roles in children's lives. I must have been in third or fourth grade when Corinne Palmer came to the small two-room country schoolhouse to teach. I knew right away that she liked me and understood me, that she thought I was cute and thought I was smart. She matched my sense of humor and my wit. When I refused to sing during music class, she kept me after school. During the next music class, I mouthed the words but made no sound. On my way out the door, heading home with my hat and coat on, I said to her, "Ha! I fooled you! I didn't really sing a word." She replied, "Then I guess you should stay after school again." She smiled at me; I was outsmarted and again stayed after school. She won. After that, I sang.

How much easier life became when we moved back in with you, Mumma. Sure you had to go to work, but we felt loved. Now here I was being cared for at home and at school! Life was good. And became even better. How excited I was when my baby sister was born at home. The first baby in our family, not counting Jibby, who was born when I was only two. To me, my new sister was the most beautiful baby alive. To my surprise, my teacher, Miss Palmer, took time to stop at my house and enjoy this miracle with me.

This teacher constantly challenged me to do creative things such as write stories, or build dollhouses out of nothing but a cardboard box and a scrap of cloth; now she was showing me she took an interest in every part of my life. Is it any wonder I have loved and do still love teaching? I know when I reach Heaven, St. Pete will say, "Take the second door on the right. There is a class waiting there for you." Meanwhile, perhaps Miss Palmer is holding down the fort.

Care and concern were shown in so many ways. There came a day when a molar made my mouth so swollen and painful that just sitting in school hurt. I cried a lot at night from the pain. This dear teacher asked my mother for permission to arrange for me to see a dentist, the closest one being ten miles away. She took me to her home after school and to the dentist the following day. The pain about killed me when the dentist pulled out my infected tooth. I screamed all the way through the extraction. If only I'd heard those words, "Run Betty, run!" I trust the years since then have brought about a better Novocain. When it was over, Miss Palmer took me to her home where her niece, Sylvia, was waiting so I would have a companion as I spent the night there recovering.

When Miss Palmer died of cancer years later, she left a little of herself living in me that was passed on to those I taught.

Pa-Man

Everyone called him Pa, but I couldn't do the same.
He was not a father to me, Dad was not his name.
There never was a real love, nor yet was there hate.
Trying to get to know him was just a bit too late.
Did he ever know my heart and did he ever care?
When I shed tears of hunger, was he ever there?
He walked out and left our house, never once looking back
Not wanting to see our pain and suffering and lack.

Pa?

Just because you didn't watch, does not remove your blame.
You were given five great kids, all bearing your name.
No doubt about it, you were wrong not to bear your load.
But God is gracious and to us, His love overflowed.
So, Goodbye Irving Groves, to a Pa I never knew.
May God bless those you've left behind, draw them closer,
      too.
Seven children still remain, each with some small part
Of a seed that came from you to give each one a start.

- Betty Williams

Chapter II

The Pa-Man

*W*e would have stayed a while longer in the children's home if our father had not pulled a sneaky move. He convinced the administrators that he had permission to take the three of us girls with him and his new wife to Massachusetts to live with them. This was certainly not an act of love, but something to hurt you, Mumma. It was as though a wicked stepmother had come to life from one of the many fairy tales I had read. Among other things, she daily harped on my neck being dirty and sent me back again and again to wash it. I bore the brunt of her cruel jokes. One day I scrubbed my neck raw; when I asked if it was clean enough to please her, she just stared at the bloody skin and never pulled that stunt again.

On my seventh birthday, my only gift was a card from you, Mumma. The quarter inside the card made me feel loved and rich; there could not have been anything better. It took just seconds to race to the store and buy an orange-flavored popsicle. After consuming the last delicious drop, I turned the stick over and there were the magic words in big capital letters, "LUCKY POPSICLE." Charley Bucket could have felt no greater thrill with Willy Wonka's golden ticket than I did with my popsicle stick as I raced back to the store to get another free popsicle. That second one was even better than the first because it made me feel that not only did my mother love me, but so did God. After all, He was the one who arranged the second popsicle.

Life on the streets of Boston was hateful. Life at the children's home had at least been organized. Rewards were given to those who did well and punishment to those who didn't follow the rules. In Boston, it was hit or miss. No one seemed to care. Rudeness was given and accepted.

Then came the unforgettable day when Mary and I were

jumping rope on the city sidewalk. I glanced up, and there you were, Mumma, coming toward us. I thought you were a vision or a dream. Mary and I ran into your open arms with laughter and tears. You whispered to Mary, "Go get your sister Jean." The four of us took a walk around the corner, and parked there on the street was a Ford car with a man in the driver's seat. This was Dominic, your new husband—never to be confused as a new father. Years later, I wondered if perhaps your main reason for marrying him was that it was your only means of getting us back.

None of those ideas entered our minds at that time, though, as the three of us snuggled down with a blanket in the rumble seat on that beautiful afternoon. I knew God was closing a chapter in my life and a new one was about to begin. It could not get any better because now my mother was close by to love and protect me.

Arriving at what was to be our new home, we finally had both love and freedom. We were gathered in a room and told that we needed to work together and to try not to fight and argue. Jean, going on fifteen, was to be in charge. We were admonished to forget the rudeness and cussing learned in Boston, but to remember the politeness we had been taught at the children's home.

Dominic was not really in our lives too much. He had been given a "hands off" order and forbidden to dole out any discipline. He was a tall, dark, and handsome man who spoke with a French accent. His spare time was spent in a rocking chair, drinking a bottle of beer, playing the harmonica, and singing. I can still hear his deep, raspy voice:

> When dey cut down dat old pine tree,
> And dey carried it away to da mill
> To make a coffin of pine
> For dat sweetheart of mine
> When dey cut down dat old pine tree.

Oh she's not alone in dat grave tonight
Wid her, my heart will always be
In dat coffin of pine
Wid dat sweetheart of mine
Where dey cut down dat old pine tree.

The squeaking of his old chair rocking back and forth kept rhythm, and harmonica notes between verses filled the air with melancholy music.

The unexpected blessing mentioned earlier—my new sister—came from this union. You, Mumma, were going through menopause, or so you thought, until that day you came back from a visit to the doctor with astounding news. Within three months we would have a new baby in our home. Jibby had considered that he would always be the baby of the family—as did we all.

Finally the day arrived, with very few preparations, when the doctor came to our house carrying his little black bag. We all had been drilled on how to act, and as ordered, came out of our bedrooms to sit quietly on the stairs. We heard no moans or groans whatsoever—amazing. The first sound was that of a baby's strong cry. We whispered in excitement but didn't move until we heard the door slam behind the doctor, at which time we rushed into the room to see a tiny bundle lying on the bed. The chocolate cake on the stand said "Welcome Joe Pete," but it should have read, "Welcome Valencia Mary." Dominic named her.

After having such plain girls' names in the family—Jean, Mary, and Betty—Valencia sounded quite glamorous. Poor Jibby had a raw deal carrying a family name: Charlmer! As his big sister, I enjoyed letting the world know his true name. "Jibby" was not much better, knowing that it came after a visit to a zoo where we met a chimp named Jibby. Nothing helped the boy. He tried to have people call him Charlie, but it didn't stick. He finally settled for Jib, which is probably the name that will appear on his tombstone. My oldest brother, Dooley, also had a name problem; his wife preferred calling him Irving all her life. When she died and Dooley remarried, his new wife, Mary, tried to help by calling him Dudy; that name stuck for the most part. My sisters and I got off lucky by comparison.

But now here was Valencia! Jean, Mary, and I would fight over who was lucky enough to get to bathe her, hold her, or rock her to sleep. I don't remember fighting over who was going to change her diaper, though. Being the youngest, I often lost out on both counts. Two years later, Meredith Mary appeared on the scene. This time we waited on the porch steps. It had been decided the hospital would be best for this birth, and now it was time for the taxi to bring you and my new sibling home. Because you knew, Mumma, of the love I had for my siblings and my desire to take care of the little ones, you placed the new blue-eyed, blonde-haired, live doll in my outstretched arms with the words, "Here, this one is for you." It was certainly meant to be, because we bonded in a way not always understood by others—a way that has lasted a lifetime.

As these two new little sisters grew, the three of us were inseparable. Once I was asked why my mother always made me take them wherever I went. I answered, "Are you kidding? She tries to keep them home, but I want them with me!" I loved these dainty live dolls, and they filled a need in my life.

* * * * *

It was quite clear that Dominic truly loved my mother, but gaining an instant family of five children the day after he was married and then adding two small girls of his own took its toll. After their divorce, I didn't miss Dominic—I never really knew him. Life for the six of us children at home did not change much. Hunger was a faithful companion, and two slices of white bread with some mustard and a piece of bologna between them was often considered a good meal.

We were given the gift of a gigantic playground, where we wandered through fields of daisies, buttercups, and devil's paintbrushes. Blueberries grew bigger and sweeter on the graves on the hillside cemetery, and no one seemed to mind that we picked them there. Sometimes we ate the berries, and sometimes we sold them for the money to go to a ten-cent Saturday matinee. This included a cartoon and an episode of Flash Gordon, as well as the main presentation. It took a complete day to pick the berries, sell the berries, and walk eight miles to the Strand Theater.

It was good protection to go in a small group, which we usually did. One day my sisters and I went to see a Shirley Temple film. Mary leaned over and whispered in Jean's ear; she and Jean then switched their seats. Suddenly, in the stillness of the audience, I heard my sister's distinct voice boom out, "Would you please remove your hand from my knee!" The man sitting beside her quickly got up, and with head bowed low, skulked out of the theater. My sister's performance was more memorable than the movie!

In the summer, our neighborhood gang came out to play cowboys and Indians in the woods where pine boughs were plentiful to build huts. We hid behind large trees and jumped out to capture each other—the Indians with crudely made bows and arrows, the cowboys with stick-guns. Gunshots were voiced by shouting "Bang! Bang! Okay, you're dead!" Late afternoons might find us sitting cross-legged on the grass in front of the house, playing Gin Rummy or Jackknife. Twilight was the time for a game of kick-the-can or a version of hide-and-go-seek. There was never a lack of something to do in our small neighborhood.

In the winter, it was different. We wandered over the hills of the nearby country club's golf course, which was unused in the winter. After climbing the steepest hill, we would come flying down on sleds, toboggans, skis, cardboard boxes, or anything else we could get our hands on. Laughter echoed all around us as we flew down in the cold, crisp air, feeling the warmth of the winter sunshine.

The links were for sliding and skiing, but the frozen bog was for ice skating. Every year at least one person would break through a spot of thin ice, but other than feeling the icy cold, no damage was done by standing in the shallow water. A blazing bonfire close by warmed tingling fingers and toes. After a few winter hours outside, it was time to go home and make hot chocolate—the first thing Maine children learned to cook on their own. We started with one teaspoon of Hershey's unsweetened cocoa and two teaspoons of sugar. Boiling water was poured over this in a mug, and lastly we added a tablespoon of evaporated milk. Never since has there been a drink invented that could compare to this; I feel sorry for children who buy pre-made drinks. What a rich, healthy place we had to grow up in!

* * * * *

It was a good thing doctors made house calls, or there would no doubt have been many more deaths in our neighborhood. There was no means of transportation for most of us. A doctor showed up only when the situation was serious, so it was frightening when he came to see me. Was I going to die? It turned out to be a simple case of tonsillitis, and my mother was told to paint the whole back of my throat with iodine every four hours. When I refused to open my mouth for this feat to be accomplished, I was promised a real Shirley Temple doll if I cooperated.

Mumma, you made good on your promise; I kept that doll for years!

Spankings were not as frequent for me as they should perhaps have been. When one took place, I had no doubt as to the reason why. I remember the hugs when it was over and the nickel to run down to Grandpa Groves' store to buy an ice cream cone or some candy. Because this was the only store within walking distance in our neighborhood, it was frequented many times in a week. My grandfather would wait on me without acknowledging in any way that we were even related. There was never a hug or a piece of candy given as a gift. His wife—not to be confused as a grandmother—treated me with a bit of disdain. She would loudly make little comments to anyone who would listen, such as, "She (referring to me) does not have naturally curly hair. Her mother puts long curls in it by using a lot of soap to keep them in place." I don't know what she was trying to prove, but the tone of voice was belittling.

I was wrongly judged by my mother only once in my entire childhood, so far as I remember. The milkman would daily deliver two quarts of milk in glass bottles. The thick cream would separate from the milk and rise to the top, pushing the cardboard lid half an inch up. In the winter, this would freeze and be true ice cream. Each night we left the clean, empty bottles out on the doorstep for the milkman to exchange for full ones. One morning, a bottle was broken, and the blame landed on me. I cried about it and was told, "A guilty conscience needs no accuser." (God, now that she is with you, please tell Mumma that I didn't do it and that I wasn't lying. Thanks!)

Postscript: probably Jibby did it.

* * * * *

Taking a bath was a ritual on Saturday nights in our house, as a preparation for church on Sunday morning. This becomes problematic when "running water" means grabbing an aluminum three-gallon water bucket in each hand and running to a spring tucked in the woods across the street from the house. After filling the buckets, the trick was to spill as little as possible going back home. The fire in the black iron stove was stoked up, and a metal tub was placed on the floor close to it. Teakettles and pans squeezed together on the top of the iron stove, hissing with the steaming water. A miniature room was built around the tub by backing the kitchen chairs up close to it and draping towels or blankets over them. This was fine, as long as you were sitting down in the warm water. At the magic moment, all the lights were turned off, and we bathed by the dim light of a kerosene lamp.

Mary hated being second in line to bathe and—rightly so—always accused me of peeing in the water when I went first. Then came one memorable winter night… Mary was much taller than I was and beginning to develop slight bumps on her chest. I waited until just the right moment for her to stand up as she scrubbed. Then I lit a few matches all together. There she stood in all her glory, and I have never seen her that angry! Consider it a miracle that I am still alive today. Her face got very red and, later, so did my bottom.

Bathing was difficult, but it did not compare to the daily inconvenience of going to the bathroom. The two-seater out in the shed was windy and cold, especially from underneath. Toilet paper was a luxury we seldom enjoyed; the Sears catalog was a must. It helped pass the time while we sat, and if scrunched in our hands until it softened, was a good substitute for toilet tissue. When tempted to complain, we heard how the poor Indians had only dried corncobs to use…and reuse… Necessity, they say, is the mother of invention.

* * * * *

Soon, social life became entwined with church life as many caring people guided our teenage group. When Pastor Ricker came to town, we no longer sat back and listened to Old Testament stories and observations on the beauty of the world around us. Pastor Ricker was a man with a purpose, having started preaching late in life. During a boring sermon, when he was just a parishioner, he had thought, "Even I could do a better job than this!" The inaudible words came back instantly, "Then why don't you?"

So he quit his electrician job and attended college to become a pastor. Now he was ready and raring to go, sharing his time between two churches. One day, when I arrived early, this man of God sat down with me and explained the way of salvation so simply that there could be no lack of understanding on my part. When he asked me if I would like to receive Jesus as my Savior, to this day I can remember my immediate thought, "If what he is saying is true, I'd be a fool not to." Right there we knelt together and, at the age of fourteen, my life changed forever. Whereas I had questioned the meaning of life, that day I found a purpose for living and knew my being in the world was no mistake because I was a part of God's plan.

Pastor Ricker helped me through my teenage years, assuring me there were no temptations I felt that were not common to everyone. Corinthians 10:13 became a great comfort. "There has no temptation taken you but such as is common to man; but God is faithful…"

He taught us to be more God-conscious, and less self-conscious. Now this is easier to say than to do when the hand-me-down clothes you are wearing are not only too large but also the worst color in the world—puke green—and make your olive skin look sallow. I would walk down the school hallways repeating over and over to myself, "God is with me. God is with me…" hoping to gain some confidence.

* * * * *

Sixteen was my favorite age to be. Life was good. Church activities kept me busy. There were church socials; I sang in the choir, played the violin in the small church orchestra, and had a job in Bates Mill. I loved everything about my home life but hated everything about school.

And then there was the war, which came without warning

to most Americans. Our lives changed overnight with the bombing of Pearl Harbor. The draft took all the young men away from us. The lyrics of one song were:

Let's remember Pearl Harbor
As we go to meet the foe
Let's remember Pearl Harbor
As we did the Alamo
We will always remember
How they died to set us free
Let's remember Pearl Harbor
And go on to victory

After two years, the lyrics changed slightly:

They're either too young or too old
They're either too fresh or too bold
What's good is in the army
What's left will never harm me.

Or:

1942 What a man!
1943 What? A man?
1944 What's a man?

I never met an unpatriotic American back then. There was great appreciation for those willing to leave their homes and loved ones to protect us from bombs coming any closer. If a military man boarded a bus, then every man, woman, and child would be willing to get up and give away their seat. Overhead baggage shelves were cleared out so tired soldiers or sailors could crawl up in them and stretch out to sleep. Our neighbors had seven sons in the service, and they were proud of it.

Every household learned to put black curtains over their

windows; and when the sirens sounded, there was a complete blackout in the land. Some foods were rationed, but this didn't affect us, as we didn't have enough money to buy even the amount allotted us.

Our only information about what was going on overseas came from the radio. Each letter coming from or going to servicemen was carefully censored to a degree where often there were more blackened squares on a page than visible words.

Train and bus stations were crowded with proud young men and crying parents and loved ones. Our happy land was now a sad one, and I remember how later in life my three year old daughter would sing the last two lines of "My country, Tis of Thee":

Land of the Pilgrims pride
Land where our fathers *cried*.

Which is so true… Many tears have been shed while maintaining freedom for this country.

Because of the war, women began to take men's jobs. I was proud to tell friends that my mother was a "Rosie the Riveter" in a shipyard. One day during that time stands out as though it were yesterday…

It was a hot afternoon, and I was cleaning the kitchen floor with an old-fashioned mop and bucket of soapy water. (No doubt I wanted to impress you, Mumma, into thinking I was a pretty good kid after all!) Suddenly, I had an urge to pray, an urge too strong to be ignored. I threw the soggy mop across the room and knelt in front of a kitchen chair. I pleaded with God to send my mother safely home. I stayed on my knees until I felt inner peace and a strong confirmation from God that He was going to take care of things. Getting up, I made note of the time.

Later that evening, as we were sharing the day's events, you told me, Mumma, of how you nearly died and how God had overruled. You had been accidentally locked in an airtight, soundproof space in a ship's bottom where you had been welding. Most workers had gone home, but God sent one man back to fetch a forgotten tool—and found a forgotten woman. On checking the timeframe, it had happened while I was on my knees. God did not forget you.

* * * * *

It was twilight…that beautiful time of day when the fireflies appear out of nowhere. The kerosene lamp was lit, and I sat patiently waiting, positioned to see the headlights of the cars from quite a distance; and as each one approached, the feeling of excitement grew. This could be the one—the one that was bringing my dear mother home from a long day's work and from far away. Oh, how I had missed her, but soon my world would be all right. I would think, "Hers will be the fifth car." I started counting—one, two, three… Then, I whispered, "Well, hers will be the next fifth car." Oh the joy when a car finally pulled up beside our home! "Mumma is home—all is well!"

Later, I wrote a deep and quite profound poem:

What's home without a mother?

It's like an outhouse without a cover—*it stinks!*

Chapter III

Leaving Home

*H*ad I known it would be my last goodbye to you, I don't think I would have left on that sunshiny day in September. Why didn't you tell me, "Betty, I need help taking care of your two little sisters, Vinnie and Sistie"? But then you hadn't said that when I went off to college two years earlier, leaving you alone with your burden. This must have been what Jesus meant when he said, "Greater love hath no man than this, that a man lay down his life for his friends." As I grew older, I learned that the one being left always hurts more than the one leaving. Forgive me, Mumma. I never should have gone so far away from you. But, I was in love and felt I should follow my man to the ends of the earth.

Sometimes a Bible school is used by parents like e-Harmony. com, as a place to send their children after graduating from high school to meet a Christian mate. It worked as such for me.

Bob and I met at Providence Bible Institute, and besides being handsome and musically gifted, Bob had a strong desire to be of service to God as a missionary. Having been brought up on the streets of Chicago, he was streetwise and had all the right words and moves to make me fall in love with him. Neither one of us had a father figure to look up to. Together we had much to learn and started out as two babes in the woods.

My quiet life became a whirlwind. Never having been outside of New England, I was amazed to learn there was a whole new world out there. Each time our jalopy stopped, Bob jumped out and wiggled a few wires, and we were off again to a new city, a new state. Having no driver's license, I was no help. I had driven once in my life though…

Growing up, we had no cars around our house; but one summer cousin Pazu came to spend a month with us and, being

16, bought his first car. He tossed the keys to me and said, "Here, Betty, you drive!" How could any ambitious fifteen-year-old resist such an offer? I slid behind the steering wheel and shoved the key into the ignition; it actually started! I looked up and Pazu was laughing at me. No way would he get the best of me! As I shifted, the car started jump-jump-jumping down the long, steep driveway. Once at the foot of the hill, the ride became smoother, and as I didn't know how to use the brakes, on I went. My brother's house couldn't be too far away, so I decided to head there.

It was a long ten miles, careening around cars that were going too slowly and at the same time avoiding oncoming traffic. My brother Dooley's face blanched as I squealed around the corner and into his driveway. He jumped out of the way and soon realized my predicament and yelled at me to turn off the key. Needless to say, it was an incident not soon forgotten...and with many repercussions. It was ten years before there was a valid driver's license in my hand!

What I remembered most about this very memorable trip to Chicago with Bob was how many times those men in blue uniforms stopped us. At first I thought my heart would pound itself right out of my body, but a thousand miles later, the frequent stops had become a new way of life.

We had a hurried marriage in Chicago. (I discovered thirty years later that it was legally invalid because the pastor had not sent the signed papers back to City Hall.) Then as newlyweds, we were on our way to New Tribes Mission in the heart of the California redwood forests. Our drive was meant to be a honeymoon, but financial stress dictated the need for taking along a paying passenger. Jim Barker was also going to missionary training; and previous to actually leaving, he was pleased at the idea of not making the trip alone. But then Bob slid behind the wheel, and for whole trip Jim screamed and held on to the door handle, ready to jump at any given moment, as carefree Bob barreled around corners, cars, and tractor trailers.

When you are twenty, you own the world and know that nothing bad will happen. It seemed like California would never reach us, but we finally connected.

It was unbelievable! Boot camp trained religious missionaries heading off into the jungles how to live the way our family had lived for many years in Maine—with no electricity, no running water, and only a woodstove to cook on. It was meant to be preparation for living and working in much less developed countries but was very familiar to me. Things like starting a fire in a wood stove were a problem for many of the future missionaries, but to me it was second nature and brought back memories.

I had come home from school to a cold house and often got up in the morning to a cold house. The only way to get warm was to make a fire. There was no other heat in our house at night, which meant snuggling under thick covers and cuddling either Jean or Mary. We were warm in the large flannel nightgowns you, Mumma, had made for us. Unheated childhood bedrooms were not a problem. Usually, when we flew down the stairs, you had a crackling fire going to greet us. We would use our large flannel nightgowns as tents and get dressed under them.

Bob, however, had not been so fortunate as I had been growing up. Our little wooden cabin in California, which was tucked in the midst of giant redwood trees, became rather chilly at night, so Bob creatively made a stove out of a metal barrel. He proudly put in paper and dry wood and then lit a match. Not much happened, so he poured a little kerosene on the wood, tossing a match in after it. Swish! The fire came up quickly, and Bob went around for days with no eyebrows or eyelashes, and the hair framing his face was slightly singed. Experience is the best teacher.

There are some advantages to not having running water. In Maine it meant having no pipes to freeze when the fire went out at night. In California it simply meant getting some good exercise. It was about the same distance to fetch water from two different places. Grabbing two tin buckets and running to fill them from a spring or brook and running back again is not traditionally a fun way to pass time. But it was life. Boot camp didn't teach me as much as growing up in Maine did. I can identify with the apostle Paul, who said "I know both how to be abased and how to abound."

There were some new things, though. Baking bread and making doughnuts were my favorites, and Bob was pleased when I learned how to do a fairly decent job of cutting his hair. But I did not care for our medical lessons. Giving injections was not my cup of tea, and the gruesome films we had to watch of childbirth made me shudder at the thought of having to preside over such things in place of a doctor in far-flung villages; I never dreamt I would actually deliver well over fifty babies, alone with no one but God and the screaming mothers. They say ignorance is bliss, and perhaps there is a bit of truth there. The more one knows, the more one is accountable for.

Food, or the lack of it, was always a problem while living in Boot Camp. There came a day when the only thing left was a large can of spinach, which had been sent to us by a church group that had organized a "clean your shelves and send it to the missionaries" day; it would have been much better had these heavy cans not been sent cash on delivery—we used every cent that could be scraped together just to pay for the package. Then it turned out to be full of canned spinach! I wanted to fill the same box with the giant pinecones that were filled with heavy pitch and seeds and send it right back C.O.D.!

Bob didn't go for that idea, and now he was patiently telling me that a large can of spinach was what God had supplied, and until we ate it, God was not about to supply anything better. Ugh! Spinach...and from a can at that! The can was opened and dumped into a pan to heat. To add insult to injury, there was a giant cockroach mixed in it. No way! Bob dutifully removed the bug before heating and eating the spinach—alone.

26

New Tribes Mission was a new and not well accepted concept in the Christian realm. The founder, Paul Fleming, had been a missionary in the Philippines and had returned to the states for medical reasons. When ready to go back, he was informed that he was no longer eligible to serve God in the field, because by then he had four children instead of three, placing him over the dependents limit. Here was an anointed man of God, about to be limited by man's imposed rules—not God's rules. Paul believed that God could, would, and wanted to use anyone who would yield to Him and that God's service should not depend on age, skin color, number of children, or financial status. Before going to New Tribes, I found it hard to sit still for a whole hour. But I sat for four or five hours listening to him and loved every minute. Paul was a powerful, spirit-filled teacher.

What a mixture of candidates were gathered in one location! There were retired couples, young people just out of high school, professional people, and on and on it went. A motto was "each one teaches one," with the belief that God-given talents should be shared. This meant that the dentist who sold his house and gave up all material possessions, desiring to bring the Gospel to those who had not yet heard it, was expected to teach this straggly bunch of missionary wannabes to pull teeth.

Which happened, and Bob took to it like a duck takes to water. The aborigines we would later work with were happy to get rid of rotting and aching teeth, and Bob was more than glad to show his prowess in numbing and pulling the teeth. It was a sight to behold. If he pulled the wrong one, he simply went back in and pulled the right one. If a tooth broke off, he would gallantly tell the owner to sit tight for a little longer while he dug it out the way he had been taught.

During these formative and vulnerable years at New Tribes, I learned many things that soon became a part of my basic philosophy. I recall being taught to speak out your true feelings to other students as to how you feel about them. This could be helpful in developing a better missionary character in both people. Being an adventurous soul, I tried it out. I approached a girl and told her honestly, "I don't know you, but I hate your guts. Every time you come into a room, I feel repulsed."

There is truth to the saying that fools walk in where angels fear to tread. She looked at me for a stunned second and then did what any honest twenty-year-old girl would do—she burst into tears. She confided to me that she knew most people felt the same way about her, even though no one had ever put it so bluntly. We cried together for awhile and then became best friends.

*****

New Tribes Mission had "Cloud Club" once a week. We all sat around in a circle, and each person was to take a turn and truthfully share how he or she was feeling. I didn't benefit as much from this as some others, as I just couldn't share too deeply. I wanted to tell them how I had tried to make fudge with Bob criticizing my every move, how the silent anger simmered deep down inside me as I desperately hoped he would stop. He didn't. The simmer rose to a boil, and I discovered a part of me I had never known—I did have some of my mother in me after all!

I stood up and slammed my large metal spoon at the wall with such force that it broke in two. I had heard somewhere that when people get mad they should count to ten, and they will feel better. I ran out of the little redwood cabin and went to a lonely spot. I counted to ten, then on to a hundred. I actually got up to five hundred, and when I stopped, I was still mad enough to kill. So much for that theory…

Remember our letters around that time, Mumma? We were making plans for you, along with Vinnie and Sistie, to join us in California. Then your letters stopped coming, and my insides felt that something was dreadfully wrong. I wanted to fly home to Maine right away, but Bob wanted more proof that such a trip was necessary than just a feeling. And so we waited. Eventually news reached us that you were in the hospital and near death.

It was too late when I finally reached your side. You were alive but in a coma. I don't think you even knew I was near. Everyone was there, but no one had contacted me. My heart was in turmoil. The brain tumor took over quickly, and you left us. Now there was grief and anger within me. Unwanted thoughts prevailed, but I kept it all inside. By the time your funeral was over, our meager funds had run out, and I found employment in a hospital for maternity cases. I saw many births and deaths of babies. I heard the loud screams of birthing pains and loud wails from mothers whose babies did not survive. It was during this time I discovered I was pregnant with Christina.

It made me feel I had to somehow hold my life together. For an inexperienced twenty-one-year-old, this was not easy…but God and I became much better acquainted. There was so much to think about on the flight back to California.

Days sped by quickly now, and with boot camp finally over we were to head back to Chicago in our old Jalopy. Bob had made a camper out of a regular car by sawing off the back half of it and putting in its place a large wooden box the size of a small cabin, where we could eat and sleep. We looked like gypsies. We had twenty-seven dollars in our pockets and a baby in my tummy. Bob said if we were going to trust the Lord for our needs in South America, we'd better do it in the States first, because it would be easier on God. Co-workers felt sorry for us. After all, I was seven months pregnant. They passed around the hat. Now we had a hundred fifty dollars, total, and could probably make it all the way…if we ate sparingly. We got into the car ready to go, with friends shouting good wishes.

But the car wouldn't start. So people stopped waving and started pushing. Finally, the car chugged, and we were off.

We didn't get very far before the generator burned out. It

cost us a hundred twenty-three dollars to get it fixed, leaving us with our original twenty-seven dollars.

We ran out of gas and money in Phoenix, Arizona. Bob was happy and excited. "Now we'll see a miracle," he said. He parked the vehicle in a location where an overhead rock jutted out, giving ample shade. He left me and took off by thumb and foot. Five hours later, he came back with good news. A construction company had hired him on the spot, and for as long as he wanted. He decided to work only one day so we would have to depend on the Lord again when the money ran out. So, with enough money for food and gas for one day, we were off again.

It was on a Sunday the next time it happened. It was a rainy, cloudy day, late in the afternoon. Bob decided we should clean up and go to church and think about what to do next. We ate a meager sandwich of peanut butter and bread and started out church hunting. We were driving around a small town when we began to notice people walking with Bibles under their arms. We followed one of them and came to a quaint interdenominational church. It was good to sing out the familiar hymns; and while we were singing, the pastor came up and talked with Bob quietly. Bob got up and preached that night. As he preached, a storm brewed outside, growing wilder until all the lights went out. You'd never know it. No one said a word. Bob kept preaching. By the time he'd finished, the lights were on again. The congregation wanted to adopt us!

They wanted us to stay until my baby was born a month down the road, but Bob felt we should move on to Chicago. I have often wondered in which direction our lives would have gone had we stayed. Mumma, you had passed on five months earlier, and here were other loving, sheltering mothers. I yearned to stay, but Bob said we had to move on.

Chapter IV

Leaving Chicago

*C*hristina was six-months old, had had all her shots, and so we figured it was time for us to move out to the mission field after living awhile in Chicago. We had made a commitment and would now fulfill it. But, where to go? South America was our destination, but we didn't know where in South America. Actually, we didn't have a preference. While reading the Bible, Bob read of how the disciples had drawn names after Judas was no longer considered one of the twelve disciples, and replacement was needed. Using this as an example, Bob figured, "If this was good enough for the disciples, it is good enough for us." We put all the names of the South American countries in a hat and drew out Venezuela. We later discovered we couldn't get visas for that country, so we obtained Bolivian visas, thinking we might be able to switch later. We ended up living mostly in Brazil.

With visas in our hands and all the required shots in our arms, we needed the wherewithal to travel. We had no money, but we decided if it were really God doing the providing, we shouldn't have to go around begging for it. By this time, New Tribes Mission had bought a plane of their own and had two good pilots. We would still be expected to pay our passage, though. As each day drew closer to leaving time, we counted not dollars, but pennies. The day arrived, and we were lacking $10. Only $10. It would have been so easy to borrow or ask for it, but we had a contract with God—if we do His work, He should supply us. We were going right to the airport and then, if $10 did not appear, Bob would go to Bolivia and get settled while Chris and I would follow later.

As our dear pastor, Lance Lathom, shook hands goodbye, he put something in Bob's hand and said, "I wish this could be more, but it is all that I have right now." It was a ten dollar bill. We were leaving the United States with an infant, a promise of $27 a month to come, and were flat broke. It would have to be from God's hand to our mouths, and I must say, He did a great job of supplying.

The plane stopped in Greensburg, South Carolina, where all twenty-six future missionaries were put up in homes of church members. We shared testimonies in their churches and were fed fried chicken morning, noon, and night and then were on our way once again. The next stop was Miami. There, the missionaries were separated, and the nineteen of us going to Brazil or Bolivia would leave first. The plane would then return to Florida and pick up the load of missionaries going to Venezuela. Our plane also landed in Quito, Ecuador, where we had precious fellowship with the small group striving to make contact with Auca aborigines. The radio station there was impressive, and I fell in love with the voice of Jean O'Delle as she sang gospel songs in Spanish.

Later, after dropping us off and picking up the second load of missionaries, the plane was heading into Venezuela for an airport where the runway lights were to be left on for them. But the lights were off. The new missionaries we had been laughing with, sharing with, and bonding with, were then no longer on this Earth. This was hard to accept. Why would such dedicated people, just starting out in true living, be swept away so suddenly? It was beyond my comprehension. "Trust in the Lord with all thine heart and lean not unto thine own understanding," the Bible says. I just had to trust that He knew what He was doing. I did, however, realize that had Bob and I obtained visas for Venezuela when we requested them, we too would have been on that plane. God had much more he wanted to accomplish through us here in this world.

* * * * *

That was a rough plane trip for us, being as broke as we were. There were snacks to buy, which did us no good. When offered to me, I would graciously smile and say, "No thanks," even though I wanted to grab it out of their hands and wolf it down. But, being a child of the depression had trained me to quietly submit to hunger. Sleeping was an easy way out, if it could be accomplished. I also spent time trying to learn a few Spanish phrases and not to confuse "tengo hambre" with "tengo hombre" or "I have a man" instead of "I have hunger." I learned quite a bit on that eleven-hour plane ride.

Paul Fleming, our mission director as well as New Tribes founder, must have had a good sense of humor. After landing in Brazil, he put us all in one small house. On one side of the Rio Negro was Bolivia, and on the other side was Brazil. Although our papers were for Bolivia, he decided that all of us should stay in Brazil. There was one American missionary family already there, whom he kindly took back to the States, lest we have someone to translate for us. Nineteen strange, English-speaking Americans all squeezed into a one-bedroom house.

There was only one other married couple. They had a child Chris's age—seven months old. We shared a bedroom with them. Bob and I had a cot smaller than a twin bed—as did the other slim couple. The babies were in jungle hammocks strung high across the room. The first time this couple had any inkling that I was not as meek and mild as I appeared to be occurred when, late in a quiet night, I shoved Bob so unexpectedly and so hard out of bed that he landed in the middle of the floor. I am not sure if the Smiths were more surprised, or if he was. He did look silly, sitting stunned in the middle of the floor. Soon we were all laughing, trying unsuccessfully not to awaken the two babies. We grew close to this couple and felt heart break when a few months later, the mother and child did not survive a plane crash. That was two crashes in a year that claimed my friends. I still hate to fly.

There was very little I could feed Chris, and we had no

money to buy milk. Every time she cried for her bottle, I gave her sugar water. As God had sent manna from heaven to the children of Israel wandering in the wilderness, I had expected manna or money from heaven, but our faith was being sorely tested. It is one thing to be hungry yourself, but it is nothing compared to seeing your child go hungry. The final blow came when Lillian, the other mother, came to me and said, "I really don't like to interfere, but don't you think you give your baby way too much sugar water and not enough milk?" My pride was shattered. I wanted to be the best mother in the world and now felt among the worst.

I longed to give my little girl the milk she needed. I went in silence, to cry for a while. A gentle tap on my door brought me back to reality. The door was shoved open a crack and there stood Lillian, who was also crying. "I am so sorry. Just now did I realize you were out of milk and money. I also have neither, but I am nursing my baby and have milk to spare. Let me nurse your baby for you." The next day a little money came in the mail from one of God's children who felt the urging of the Holy Spirit to send it. God delayed provision just long enough for me to learn a few lessons about love and bonding.

In that foreign country, there was no welfare, no food kitchens, nor even trashcans to raid. When you're out of food… you're out of food! I have never heard of a faith missionary starving to death. I have heard of those who left when life got tough, and I often wondered how they came up with the two or three thousand dollars for the trip home.

Nineteen grown people and two babies trying to live together in a small place is true stress. There were few supplies, not much food, and single young men can dispose of food fast! Little things started to irritate, like when we all chipped in to buy a stalk of bananas. David Yarwood would always eat them green, so none ripened for the rest of us. David was a large and even-tempered, happy man; and if I had approached him, he would gladly have helped solve the problem of having no bananas for the babies. Years later, when the aborigines took David's life, I was to reflect on our days together and felt privileged to live under the same roof with this Godly giant.

* * * * *

There was laughter and fellowship as we rattled around. A Brazilian pastor offered to teach us Portuguese. When one of us pulled on our ear lobe and proudly declared, "lapis, lapis," he never cracked a smile, even though calling our ear a pencil was funny. We laughed, though, and forever after called our ears, pencils. Worse yet, was when a missionary made a pineapple-upside down cake to share with the Portuguese class after a lesson. A student was studying the top of the cake that had melted brown sugar mixed with pineapple lumps and coconut. She wanted to show her progress in the language and pointed to this brown squishy mixture as she told the pastor, "Parece coco."

But she put the accent in the wrong place; instead of saying, "It looks like coconut," she had loudly declared that, rather, "It looks like shit." Which it truly did. Again, there was not even a hint of a smile on the pastor's face as he helped himself to a large slice. I thought of him years later when I tried to teach a Spanish class how to speak English. I couldn't hold back my smile as a student made a funny mistake. One little senhora told me, "You are supposed to teach us, not laugh at us!" I should have learned this lesson years ago from that wise man of God.

In the cramped dorm-like home where we stayed, we had been blessed by inheriting the services of a fourteen-year-old maid. When she was outside on a black night, all you could see were the whites of her eyes unless she smiled—then you saw her teeth, too. She was a typical teenager and hated doing dishes. So I cashed in on this and made a bargain. I would wash the dishes, and she would wipe them while she taught me to sing in Portuguese. I still remember the words to the many songs she taught me, and now I've come to understand their meaning also.

Bob was antsy to start preaching—if not to aborigines deep in the jungle, then to the Brazilians around us. This presented a slight problem due to the communication barrier, but Bob was undaunted and went to the most public place he could find and sat down. As he started reading his Portuguese Bible aloud, many helpers stopped to give the seemingly dumb American the right pronunciation of the words. After pronouncing the words correctly, the Brazilians would try to explain their meaning. All Bob had to do was sit and listen while the Bible was read aloud and interpreted.

Across the river from us was Bolivia; and because we had Bolivian legal papers, not Brazilian papers, we moved there. We found one room with a bath right next door to a small Seventh Day Adventist hospital. The room was crowded for the three of us—Chris, Bob, and me—and became more crowded when Bob invited a nineteen-year-old Bolivian girl to live with us for reasons unknown to me at the time.

The hospital was a fascinating place to me for its primitiveness, and it was amazing what Dr. Botsford, the only doctor, was doing with so little to work with. One day he came to get me. "Come on," he said, "your baby was born by Caesarean, as will be any others in the future. You should watch what is done to you after they put you to sleep!" Here was a doctor with a warped sense of humor.

There were only three of us in the little space used as an operating room—the mother-to-be, the doctor, and me. The doctor put a cloth over the pregnant girl's nose and dropped drops of chloroform on it. Now and then he checked on the dilation of her eyes and talked to her. When he was satisfied that she was completely out, he started cutting with a sharp knife. It was so fascinating to me that I had no fear or bad feelings while watching. Giving birth is always a miracle, and no matter how often I see it, I want to cry.

He pulled a baby boy out of her bloody abdomen. Then this doctor kept up a running commentary with such statements as

"...nice, healthy kid. It's her third so I may as well tie these tubes. She can't afford any more. Look, here's the appendix. We'll remove it while we have the chance. She lives so far upriver she'd never make it if it burst." He showed me various internal parts so I would not lack in information. He also felt it would be a nice thing to clip away a lot of fat from the thick layer in her stomach, and perhaps she would feel better about herself. The mother and baby survived, and even more amazing to me at the time, I also lived through the experience.

This was the same doctor friend who felt sorry for me because I had a horrible tooth ache when there was no dentist within hundreds of miles. My swollen, painful cheek pushed him to make me an offer. He declared that although he was not a dentist, he felt he would be a good substitute. He did such a good job injecting the Novocain that it did not hurt when he extracted the tooth. Only one problem remained—he pulled the wrong one. He made things right by going back in and yanking out the problematic one.

As our missionaries had no given assignments, with God's help we were to make a nook for ourselves somewhere in the large and exciting country of Brazil. Two families had invited us to join them upriver as they were trying to make contact with a tribe of aborigines.

It took three weeks to go up the river by chug boat. Christina had just turned a year old and was active and curious. Her golden blond curls made her a hit with the dark-skinned native people. "Oh, Sheer-lee Tam-pull," they would say, admiring her chubby cuteness. Hammocks were hung in all directions. Under the five steps going below deck, a large anteater was chained up. Its tongue was a long sliver, but it was no danger. However, its claws were vicious as it reached out to grab anyone brave enough to climb the stairs. Pigs ran loose on deck, and chickens couldn't go too far because their legs were tied together. There were sacks of rice and sacks of dried beans. Kerosene was being shipped upriver in five-gallon square cans. We arranged these cans to make a playpen for Chris. It served the purpose and kept her safe and happy.

There was strong, sweet coffee for breakfast, and rice and beans for dinner, and rice and beans for supper every day. At first it tasted so good; but then it seemed I would rather starve to death than eat any more—sort of the way I felt about oatmeal when I was living in the children's home. About this time, the men pulled the boat as close as they could get to shore. I couldn't swim, but I didn't care if I drowned—I needed to get off that smelly boat! I jumped into the river with its piranhas and strange color and dog-paddled to shore beside Bob, who swam with Chris clinging to his neck. The men dug up dozens of turtle eggs that looked like ping-pong balls and were almost all yolk on the inside.

Our group caught a turtle about two feet in diameter, and the boatmen cooked it over an open fire, using the shell as a cooking pan. It was the only way to do it, as that old turtle was reluctant to give up his shell, but after an hour or two over the fire, he didn't care anymore. Everyone sat around his big shell, and reached in to grab a hunk of turtle meat, which had been sprinkled with a little farinha.

We arrived in Cafetal and were given a little room of our own to sleep in. We were to eat one week with one family and one with another, until we could get settled. The walls and floors of this room were made of red sweet mud clay, and Christina thought it was like a gingerbread house that should be eaten. Life became much easier when Bob built her a combination high chair and potty chair, though she was never quite sure which function was to be utilized when. He also built a screened-in playpen bed, against her objections. At night, she demanded I lean over the tall screen so as to hold her hand and sing until she dozed off. I think my right arm is now a good bit longer than my left.

We bathed and washed our dishes and our clothes in the river close by. The best way was to stay close to shore or in the old boat docked there, as the piranhas did not appreciate our intruding on their territory. These man-eating fish do make a tasty meal, however. Days were hot, buggy, uneventful, and slow. Cafetal was on the Bolivian side of the river, but it would have been the same had it been in China—we could not communicate with the few people living there. So, when a young girl with hair flying in the wind came running in frenzy up to another missionary woman and myself, gesturing that she needed us to help deliver a baby, it broke life's monotony. One of the other missionaries and I grabbed a how-to book and tried to refresh our memories of films on how to deliver babies that had been shown in missionary boot camp—the films I had been so reluctant to watch.

The girl led us to a mud hut tucked away a bit farther upstream. The screams could be heard long before we reached the door. "Yo no puedo, yo no puedo. Yo quiero mama!" "I can't do this," the new mother was screaming. "I want my mother!" As we entered, I thought, "Yeah? Well, so do I!" We were both, the expectant mother and myself, around twenty-one; perhaps the song "She's a young thing and should not leave her mother" had some truth in it for both of us.

Now we were a team—two missionary women who knew nothing about delivering another woman's child, but were soon to learn. We discovered that it is hard to see the baby coming when the mother-to-be is standing on the bed jumping up and down, and it is hard to concentrate on anything with chicken lice swarming over your bare legs. We found that the book on child delivery was useless to us, as we had none of the things we were told to use and no cooperation from the mother. Sometimes things happen not because of us, but in spite of us. Her beautiful, gooey baby girl was no exception.

* * * * *

Cafetal was a starting off point for Bob and me, and we

lived with two older missionary couples. Unintentional as it may have been, I felt like a misfit and a third thumb living with these two experienced women who were much older than I and also were best friends.

Our reason for being in that remote area was to reach out to savages living farther up the river and bring them the gospel. With this in mind, Bob and two other missionary men took off in a small motorboat for a three-day journey upstream. Besides food and hammocks, baubles were taken along to offer up as gifts to leave along the jungle path to indicate friendliness. Their problem, though, was that they didn't recognize the signs of unfriendliness left along their way—arrows deliberately stuck with points down all along the way, silently saying, "We don't want you. Get out of here."

Finding a spot on the river bank that showed signs of habitation, the boat was run aground and then carefully hidden in the thick underbrush—it would be a long swim back, should the boat disappear. Starting down a well-trod trail, they left their baubles—junk jewelry and tin cans—all along the way, as a way of saying, "Hello, we are here. We like you." By daylight, the men cooked, ate, and slowly pushed ahead. At night, very little sleep was had as fear was prevalent. Their zipped-tight jungle hammocks kept out bugs and snakes, but not poisoned arrows.

The men joked about one of the missionaries stage-whispering in the middle of the night, "I smell a, (and he lowered his voice as he carefully spelled out the next word) b-a-r-b-a-r-o," the Brazilian word for a savage. This became a well-used quote. Did this guy think the savages understood Portuguese? But couldn't spell it, perhaps? Fear makes one do strange things.

On the third day, Bob was feverish and weak. So after a brief discussion, it was decided the two others would go on ahead for a few more hours and let Bob sleep it off. No one wanted to give up before contacting savages, after all the time and energy put in. Bob dozed for awhile, but woke up when he heard what was thought to be his companions breaking through the brush.

40

He peered out of his screened-in hammock to see the black, shiny skin of two muscled aborigines, wearing only loincloths. The movement attracted the attention of these two fierce-looking men, and they raised their bows and arrows, pointing them at Bob, who was now in a big dilemma. If he unzipped the hammock to get out, would this noise make them shoot? What if he did nothing?

He sat quietly, trying to keep eye contact. They chattered to each other and then quietly disappeared into the tangled jungle. The question was, were they going to get their friends? Or were they leaving? Bob's sickness fled, and he jumped out of the hammock swiftly. His first act was to make a circle of baubles all around him so his good intentions would not be questionable, and then he sat down to write a farewell letter to me, which is still around somewhere. Then he simply watched, listened, and prayed. Upon the return of his friends, who had by then discovered the inverted arrows, all three made a fast retreat from the area, happy to find the boat still tucked away in its hiding place.

* * * * *

After a year or so in Cafetal, we returned to our starting point in Brazil. Being young, pregnant again, and toting a toddler, plus living in the backwoods of a foreign country, is already not the best situation to be in; but my nausea was different on one morning. No need to call the practitioner hanging around the area, I thought—that had been tried when I was doubled over with stomach pains. He had come in, poked my tummy a bit, and declared that I needed to use a suppository to clean out my system. When he stepped outside for a minute, my curiosity got the best of me. Walking very quietly, I went to his little black doctor's satchel and opened it up. Inside it was his lunch. He must have carried the satchel for show, much like some illiterate aborigines who want to show they are Christians carry a Bible tucked under one arm.

No, I was alone. Bob appeared helpless also, and before long I started to violently puke. As a foot-long white string came out and landed with other goodies on the floor, I said, "Look, Bob. Spaghetti!" Bob's slow sense of humor rose to the surface as he replied, "Look again, Honey. It's moving." Watching that white worm squiggling on the floor brought up what little had remained in my stomach. No suppository would be needed to clean me out that time...

* * * * *

From the start, we knew the baby in my tummy would have to be delivered by caesarean. It would be only ten months from the time Christina was born to the second baby's arrival, so we expected complications. Having been in Brazil only three months, we had not had enough time to discover our options for places to give birth. Our visas were for Bolivia, and this limited our choices further. We finally went to Cochabamba, Bolivia, not realizing it was almost impossible to administer anesthesia to an expectant mother in a high altitude city such as this without the anesthesia reaching the baby before it could be taken from the belly.

So the doctor there decided to freeze my stomach and take the baby that way. We had waited too long, though, as the incompetent doctor felt the labor pains should be further along before we started. As the stretcher was being wheeled down the hallway to the primitive operating room, my shivering cold body writhed with labor pains. Soon needles were being injected into my stomach, but each time the doctor made a slit, I jumped. He felt that chances had to be taken and ether given. When he came out of the operating room, Bob could hardly believe the sight of this butcher. He was covered from head to toe in blood—my blood.

When I awoke from the anesthesia, our little Elizabeth was

brought in and placed in my arms. She was beautiful, like her sister had been. I held her close to my heart and dozed again. My next awakening was to the loud noise of stillness. I felt a strong presence of God and an inner knowledge that He had taken Elizabeth home to be with Him. Then, in the twilight shadows of the unlighted room, there was a glowing white light in one corner, and I physically felt a blanket of love going over my whole body from the top of my head to the bottom of my feet. I felt a quiet peace flood over me.

I wondered if God had been trying to prepare me all along for this: strangely enough, the night before, when we left for the hospital, I looked at my beautiful two-year-old sleeping peacefully and, for some reason, I prayed aloud, "God, I really want both of my children, but if you must take one, let it be the new one because my heart is already so wrapped up in Christina, and I don't yet know the other one." These things were strange to me. Did God take me at my word? Was my fear of losing one of the children a normal reaction from living so close to death in the villages?

How did you feel, Mumma, when your tiny son was taken from you? At nineteen years of age, how did you cope? Was two-year-old Dooley a consolation? Did you know God well enough to draw on His grace and strength? Why didn't you share with me what it was like? I know where that baby's little unmarked grave is in the same cemetery that now holds your remains. Are Elizabeth and your baby boy, Lawrence, with you now? Will I know them when I get there?"

Chapter V

A New Journey

In a few short weeks we were on our way, along with another young missionary couple, to a spot on the Rio Negro to work with the Nhambaquari aborigines. This time there were no experienced missionaries to guide us and no privacy whatsoever. The few children who roamed around spent most of their time peering at us through the cracks left between the slender trees used to make our primitive little house.

Here we were as two semi-compatible missionary families in this otherwise man-forsaken land. Nhambaquari aborigines lived up the river, and we longed to bring Jesus to them, but God was perhaps more concerned that we bonded closer with the other family. Al and Alberta were from Altoona, Pennsylvania, and were too shy to speak to anyone outside our house. When curious eyes peeked at us through the wide cracks in the walls to see what these odd looking strangers were doing, it became a difficult situation for all involved.

A small sunbeam in our dark setting was the trip down river to get supplies. Even though it meant riding a whole day on a barge with pigs, chickens, large balls of raw rubber, and other passengers in a crowded space, it was worth it. The second day of our journey was easier because it was on a Smoking Mary train. Hot sparks would fly in through our open window, burning holes in our clothing. Sweaty bodies and loud talking were now a pleasure to be around—we were with people once again. The third day was the best, as missionaries met us with hugs, and two days of glorious fellowship began. These trips every two months were like Christmas. We certainly were celebrating Christ's birthday as well as His life and resurrection. But then it was all ruined.

The early morning found me packing clothes and ironing.

It was a chore to get heat from the charcoal iron. I blew, fanned, and swung the iron around and around. As smoke poured from the small chimney, enough heat was produced to iron clothes. No sacrifice was too great. Then the unbelievable happened—Al and Alberta appeared at our bedroom door and asked Bob if we would mind if they went for supplies instead. The nerve of them to ask for the one thing I looked so forward to…and of my husband for saying it was no problem without even consulting me. Their small family bustled out the door and down to the river. Their four-year-old Joel and our Christina were the same age. Their six-month old baby boy had been born a week after our little Elizabeth. She had her baby; I didn't have mine.

Drizzle darkened the sky, making two o'clock in the afternoon feel like seven at night. Anger boiled inside me, but I kept a good missionary profile. My gloomy mood matched the day. Being stuck in a small forlorn settlement consisting of a few scattered palm bark houses wasn't much help. Now and then a few grungy, skinny men stopped here in this town for a supply of liquor, on their way upriver to milk the rubber trees. It reminded me of the way sap was drawn from maple trees in New England. Instead of boiling the rubber liquid down, it was dripped onto a rotating stick over an open fire—sort of like a pig roasting on a spit. When the ball of rubber was around ten feet in diameter, it was cooled and shipped downriver on a barge. This was also a perfect way to smuggle out diamonds. Who could pull apart pure rubber to check it out?

One way to forget your problems is to find someone more miserable than you are and get involved in helping them. With this in mind, I choked back my angry tears and went into the so-called kitchen. The thatch half-walls kept no one and nothing out, but this was the place where we kept our food in covered cans and cooked on an open fire. Hanging on the center pole of the room was a cracked mirror. Before I went into the village, I wanted to see if my tears were well hidden when surprise—I saw in the mirror Alberta and her family. They had missed the boat, and a sadder and more dejected-looking family has yet to be seen.

My anger vanished. After hugging and consoling them, we joined in a nice breakfast together. Alberta handed me her baby, simply saying, "He's sick. Real sick. He won't eat and he upchucks everything we give him. I don't know what to do." The fragile baby was placed in my arms. Although children had always been special to me, not much of my time had been spent with that one—I didn't want Alberta to consider the thought that I might want to fill the hole in my own heart by taking over her baby. Now, cradling this little bundle in my arms, it was as though the word *death* was written all over his dear little face with the thin blue lips. The pent-up tears flowed freely from my eyes. Hands gently took the baby from me. The other three felt I was being paranoid…but God had taken my baby and now He was to take this one. I knew it and could not be consoled.

Less than four hours later, Bob was making a tiny coffin out of every scrap of wood he could scrounge. I lined it with a soft flannel baby blanket, unused by its intended owner, Elizabeth. The white clouds and tiny lambs on the blanket seemed appropriate. Dressing the baby boy in a soft blue flannel bunting was like dressing a cold wax doll.

Mumma, did you also have to dress your baby boy when you put him in that small coffin? Did you bury him yourself in his unmarked, tiny grave? Many times I have stood by his small cross, wondering what my brother would have been like, had he lived. Did you have loving arms around you to hold you? I wish I could have shared your burden.

Ours was a sad procession that walked to the cemetery with a tiny, rough wooden box, carried by the grieving couple. The rain fell softly from the gray clouds and a gloomy atmosphere prevailed. We were all so young and felt so forsaken and all alone. There was no howling or wailing—just the stunned questioning, "Why, God…why?"

* * * * *

It was just five months after Elizabeth's short stay on Earth that a new pregnancy for me became apparent. The plan was to leave the villages when I was in my seventh month. Having had two previous cesarean births put me at risk with this third pregnancy, and being close to a hospital was imperative. Bob and Al had gone upriver in a tiny boat to try to make contact with an unfriendly tribe of aborigines. Already, they were a week beyond their expected return, and I was due to leave because of my health. But should I wait for Bob, or should I go on? Alberta and I sought God's guidance, coming to the conclusion that I should leave on the next available barge heading out, as it came so infrequently.

It was sad, seeing Alberta and her two children waving goodbye to Christina and me as they stood on that lonesome riverbank, but it felt so good after our two-day journey to be welcomed into the group of missionaries. For two weeks in the new town, I explained to those who would listen about Alberta being left alone and how extra difficult it would be if something had actually happened to our husbands. Even though I offered to pay for the trip, none of the men in the mission home felt led to go to her aid. Finally, my burden was so heavy that there seemed no other way but to go back myself. With Christina in tow, and my very pregnant belly popped way out, I boarded the train to begin my long journey back. But God has His people everywhere; and just before the train started, a dear Brazilian lady showed up and placed her eleven-year-old son in front of me.

She said, "I have no money to offer, nor anyone I can send in your place, but I want you to take my strong son with you. He can be a protection for you, and he can carry Christina or packages. Use him to run errands or to help in any way. God has shown him that this is what he must do." It reminded me of the widow's mite and how God blessed the small gift given because she had given all she had.

The look on Alberta's face when I walked through the door was sufficient reward for all I had gone through to make the journey. We hugged each other and cried together. We had no idea what we should do next, so we tried to hire a man to make the trip upriver; but no one was willing, even for money, to go beyond a certain point because of the aborigines. It was well known that Bob and Al had gone beyond that safe point.

And so we waited and prayed, and prayed and waited. Rebecca, in my womb, let me know she was getting ready to make her entrance into the world.

News came that a barge was coming in to pick up some balls of raw rubber in a week. A decision needed to be made, so again Alberta and I sat down and went over the "what ifs." The men's situation would not be changed, regardless of what we did, outside the realm of prayer. But the baby's birth could be changed by being close to a hospital. I made plans to leave on that barge. Two nights before the date of departure, I had a very realistic dream. Bob, with a long beard and hair of six weeks' growth, along with Al, came right into the kitchen through the back door. They had an old skin-and-bones crone with them. When I awoke, the dream had been so real that I looked around for the three of them. Later in the morning, as Alberta and I prepared breakfast, the kitchen door opened, and my dream was brought to life. In they walked.

The old lady with them was close to death and was carried to a relative's house and laid out on a pallet. Bob told me to stay by her while he went in search of medicine. Maria, the niece, and I watched the shallow breathing of the body in front of us as we chatted. Suddenly, I saw the breathing stop. I felt for a pulse on the wrist of the lifeless form. There was none. "She's gone," I said.

"What do you mean, *gone?*" Maria shouted.

"She's dead," was my calm response." No, no…no!" Maria shouted in frenzy. "There are no candles lit! She was a wicked,

wicked woman who practiced witchcraft. Her evil spirit could rise from her body and go into you or me!"

She ran out of the room to look for candles. I looked down at the old, wrinkled face when, to my surprise, she opened her eyes wide and fixed her gaze on something over my head. Her face wrenched up in a twisted grimace with a look of absolute horror. I don't know what she saw, nor do I ever want to see it. If I hadn't believed in Hell previously, I most certainly would have lost all doubt just then.

That death was in stark contrast to the ones I had seen earlier, including that of an elderly Jewish lady I had been caring for. She passed away in the hospital with me by her side. A nurse made note of the time of death and left the room to contact relatives. This small lady had films over her blind eyes; but when she opened them one last time, they were clear blue, and she could definitely see something or someone above me. As she stared up, a look of peace and contentment flooded her face, and as she again closed her eyes, there was a gentle smile on her lips. I would like to have seen what she saw. Perhaps someday I will.

* * * * *

Our family left the following day, heading for a hospital in Anápolis, Brazil, a hospital run by an English doctor. As soon as we arrived, the doctor told me I should stay in the hospital, in bed, with my feet elevated to keep the baby a while longer in my tummy. Even then I might lose her, he warned, as she was so tiny. My second caesarean had been so poorly done that I was told there was a danger with this third one. The doctor said that the baby could push open the poorly done operation and push into my stomach should I go into labor; but the baby was too small for them to take surgically right then, so I should do everything possible to keep her in my womb.

Chris was only three years old and hated being away from me. Oh, the blessedness of Brazilian hospitals. A cot was brought in for her and also a few toys. We spent so many happy hours reading, playing, and just talking. She filled my lonely days. I was not to get up even to go to the bathroom. After two weeks, I found I was too weak to get up. This frightened me, so when all was quiet, in the middle of the night, I would very cautiously get up and walk around the room once or twice to maintain strength in my legs.

Christmas came. It was meager. Our money had not caught up with us for months. From experience I had learned that every time we collected a large amount of money, the need for it would arrive simultaneously. I tried to squelch these foreboding thoughts, though. After Christmas, Bob took Chris with him to the missionary home where a conference was going on. The doctor told me he planned to take the baby on January 7. So I waited, and waited, and waited…without a radio or television. I read a little, slept a lot, and prayed a lot. Then, in the early evening of December 31, I felt something. The doctor was called in before he planned to leave for a New Year's Eve party and decided to take my baby out first so he wouldn't be disturbed just when the party got rolling.

Thus, Rebecca Gail came into the world on December 31 instead of January 1.

I was cold, alone, and scared, as they wheeled me down to the operating room. It was 9:00 pm. In my church in Chicago, they would be having a New Year's service until after midnight. The music would be special, the speakers would be dynamic, and the food would be delicious. I wondered if, in all this merriment, there would be one person anywhere praying for me. I felt not. Once again I prayed, "Well God, it's just the two of us against the world. But Your grace is sufficient for me. I commit myself into Your hands."

The day after my operation, I vomited nonstop. Each time the doctor would say, "If she vomits again, we'll give her something for it." I did. He didn't. The one thing I wanted desperately was you, Mumma. I needed your arms around me and your smiling voice telling me everything would be all right. By the second day, my system had quieted down. Then I asked, "Where's my baby?"Answers were evasive, so I assumed she had died and no one wanted to tell me. After all, that had happened with Elizabeth. So I gingerly climbed out of bed, holding on to my twenty-two stitches. Nurses came on the run. "What are you doing?" they blurted.

"I'm going to see my baby!" I screamed in Portuguese. They hurried me back to bed, and I told them they had one hour before I tore the place apart. Within an hour, a small bundle was placed on my bed. No one had told me that my baby had a cleft lip and cleft palate. In spite of this, she was beautiful and quite surprising with her black, straight hair. My other two, Christina and Elizabeth, had blond wisps, and I just assumed Rebecca Gail would have the same. She was unbelievably tiny, and I knew she was a premature birth without an available incubator. I quickly counted her fingers and toes, amazed at her beauty. Then I wondered, "How will she eat?"

The doctor came and talked with me. In Brazil, there were no means to feed a child like her, and he intimated it might be better if she didn't live. I saw red. He had been passing her around to nurses, then from mother to mother; and when I talked with them, I discovered they hadn't been able to get much milk into her—only a few drops. I was desperate because this child was languid, and I thought she no longer felt hunger pains. She didn't even cry. I offered up a quick prayer, asking God to help me know how to save my baby's life, and I then took action by sending someone out to buy a hand breast pump.

The nurses came to take the baby back to the nursery. Talk about mother hens—my feathers were ruffled. "Over your dead bodies," I told them. In desperation, they called the doctor, and he told them to leave me alone. He didn't think the baby would live anyway. Then came a mother's vigil. I fed Rebecca for ten minutes every half hour, drop by drop with the milk pumped from my breast. I did this all through the night and into the next day.

Bob arrived with Christina, and we decided to leave the hospital and move into a boarding house almost across the street. I would have to return to have the stitches taken out of my stomach when the baby was five days old. Meanwhile, we could concentrate on caring for our wee one. I cried nonstop the first time I bathed her. She was smaller than a doll.

Now I knew why God had held up our money. It came in one lump sum, enough to pay for all of us to return to the States. The problem was, we were in interior Brazil and our papers were all for Bolivia. We were in the country illegally and could be in a lot of trouble. Now we had a new daughter to add to our passports; and a baby born in Brazil was a Brazilian, which she would forever consider herself to be. All in all, our papers were a mess and seemed to take forever to straighten out. Meanwhile, I wrote to major cities all over the U.S. to find the best plastic surgeons. More than one responded, and they all indicated one of two men: one at Children's Hospital in Boston and the other in Harrisburg, Pennsylvania.

Rebecca was almost six months old before we could get out of the country. I had been advised that it was best to perform her surgery within her first month. But there she was, six months old. I had noticed a two-year-old little girl running around grasping a bottle with a large hole in the nipple; and I thought, "If they can do that for a healthy child, I can certainly do it for a sick one." I bought six nipples and experimented. I gauged the hole so that it took Becky half an hour to drink her bottle. She had no suction, but by pushing up the soft nipple, it slowed the milk flow and satisfied her sucking instincts. I found a Brazilian baby cereal, "Farinha Lacta," which was a lot like Pablum in the States. Thickening the milk with it added vitamins, and her health improved.

By now, the shape of our daughter's lip was obvious, and people would stare and make comments. For the long trip back to the States, I fixed up a basket that suited our needs just fine. It made a soft bed, and it was a neat way to carry Rebecca's diapers and clothes under the small comforter.

After landing in New York, before catching a plane to Boston, I had changed and fed the baby and burped her, but I felt frustrated to see people staring at my girl. It was hard to ignore their rudeness. I had put my sleeping baby in her basket on the chair beside me, when a large lady came in a direct line over to us. She leaned over the basket, picked up the baby, holding her a little distance from her own face, and said in a loud, clear voice, "Why she is beautiful, and she is perfect because she is just the way God made her and sent her to you." She kissed Rebecca and put her down.

Then she said, "You must be very special people for God to have entrusted the care of this little one to you. What a privilege He has given you." Before I could speak, she had melted back into the crowd. Unrestrained tears flowed down my cheeks. I have prayed for God's blessing on this sweet stranger. I wish I could find her and thank her.

Arriving in the States brought only the beginning of Becky's treatments and surgeries. The first operation closed the slit that went from her upper lip to her nose. My contacts with plastic surgeons, made while still in Brazil, paid off—at Boston Children's Hospital we were welcomed into the office of a physician considered to be one of the top three specialists in the country. After a consultation with him, the nurse took us aside to set a date for the operation and talk about finances. She explained that the hospital was connected to a medical school and that some of the students would be present during the process.

I reacted quickly, jumping to my feet and declaring, "No way. No students are going to operate on my baby after I have gone through so much to get the best for her. You can be sure I will pay, even if it takes the rest of my life." The nurse beckoned me to a more secluded spot and told me, "If I said the top surgeon was going to do the operation for free, as long as students are allowed to watch, every patient in the waiting room, rich or poor, would jump at the chance. The doctor feels you are a worthy cause and wants to do this for you. If anyone asks, I will deny telling you, but I felt you needed to have peace of mind." It sure helped.

Not only was it hard on us to see our small baby wheeled out on an operating table, but Becky's reaction was unexpected. She was mad! When we were allowed to bring her home from the hospital, both her arms were in splints to keep her from doing damage or pulling out the stitches. She glared at Bob and me, but then she saw Christina and held out her tiny-splinted arms and laughed and giggled. A happy big sister gathered her baby sister into her arms and triumphantly marched out of the hospital ahead of us.

The surgeon must have been tops, because the same month Becky had been born, a member of our church in Chicago had a baby girl born with the same problem. This family had enough money and insurance to afford the best of care, and the operation took place before the baby was a month old. As mothers, we were anxious to compare notes, so on our first time back to the North Side Gospel Center in Chicago, this mother approached me, wanting to see Becky. Because of the people welcoming me home along the way, it was a while before I joined up with this perplexed mother again; she had been looking for Becky in the nursery. She said, "I have looked at every baby in here, and none has had this plastic surgery." She was wrong—Becky was right there in plain view.

* * * * *

The next major operation, concerning her cleft palate, was to be done when Becky was close to three and would require a long healing time. Two slits would be made in the flesh covering two bones in the roof of her mouth. The flesh would be stretched and pulled until it could meet in the center, edges cut to facilitate growing together. This was the equivalent of three large cuts in the roof of her mouth.

Once again we performed extensive research to find the best qualified doctor to perform the procedure, and this took us to Harrisburg, Pennsylvania. We would need to be in the area for quite a while, and God had provided us with a small camper to haul behind our Chevy. Arriving outside the town, we began to look for a place to camp. While searching, a wrong turn (or so we thought) was made. Very cautiously, we backed into the driveway of what appeared to be an empty house. Turning around with a trailer in tow is not an easy task.

Suddenly, a bosomy Italian lady came running out of the house to greet us. She thought we were company for her and decided we indeed were just that. She insisted that we park the camper under a big shade tree, close by a duck pond on her land. Then she insisted we have dinner every night with her and her husband. Wow! It was my first taste of real Italian cooking and Italian hospitality, being given to us by complete strangers. I never knew there was such a thing as actually making pasta at home!

Sitting around the feast spread out on the dinner table each night, we were kept laughing by their stories of *when we first got off the boat from Italy...* Not only were they homeless when they arrived, but also they could speak no English. The starving man became so hungry that he went to a drug store to ask where he could buy food. He did this by rubbing his tummy and opening his mouth wide while pointing inside it. After swallowing the laxative the pharmacist insisted on giving him, he spent the next day at a river's edge, washing himself and his only set of clothes. Living with this gracious Italian family was God's way of lightening our load, and oh, how we needed it.

The vision of tiny Becky standing behind the glass door in the hospital, sadly waving goodbye, remains with me still. For years I kept the tiny blue chenille robe she was wearing, as a reminder of God's goodness. Going back to the small camper and leaving her was a sad moment; and after singing Christina to sleep, I decided to stay up all night and pray for Becky. Bob had to return to Chicago, as he had a construction job at the time. Here I was, trying to be like Moses. As long as he kept his hand up, the Red Sea parted, and the children of Israel passed through safely on the dry ground. Was my incessant praying going to help Becky pass through safely? Even when God gave me peace in my heart, I was afraid to stop praying. This was like a rosary without the beads.

The doctors were not sure if another operation was going to be needed later on to lengthen the uvula in the back of Becky's throat, or if they would need to provide her with a plastic one. Again, I turned to prayer. By then Becky was talking and forming bad speech habits. She had to relearn how to talk by my taking her to speech therapy, which was held in a small room in Northeastern University. Sixteen other children were there with their mothers, and never had I seen so many deformed children in one place. I said, "No, Lord. This will not do. Help me to find a better way."

There were many books on correcting speech impediments in the college library, so I went home well armed. Becky was not pronouncing her t's or hard c's and g's, among other sounds. This became a family project, and even five-year-old Chris became a teacher. "Becky, say chree (tree)," she would say, "like in choo-choo train."

"Ch, ch, ch," Becky always tried. We all watched for small improvements, but a large one came one evening when Becky was in her crib, fussing because no one else was in bed. Soon she stopped, and all was silent until her little voice was heard in the darkness of her room. "Go away. Go away!" she called. The miracle we had been waiting for had happened. If she could pronounce a hard g, that meant all the other sounds would follow.

* * * * *

There were other trips to Harrisburg. Our camper was gone by then; and while we were in the hospital for Becky's treatment, the nurse on duty noticed we had given a Chicago address. "Where are you staying while you are here?" she asked Bob. Not wanting to admit that we had no place and no money, Bob just answered, "We are not sure yet." That was most certainly an understatement. "Well, I'm sure," she said." You are coming home with me!"

This beautiful Christian family, Smith and Lydia B, had a fourteen-year-old daughter and a nine-year-old son when they welcomed us into their beautiful home and insisted we stay each time we had to return to Harrisburg. God has His people (and angels) everywhere, and our family was living proof that God supplies all needs and then some.

*****

Illness seemed to follow Becky around. She had been in and out of hospitals all her life. When, at the age of ten, she contracted a very high fever, we prayed over her; and when the fever broke and she soaked the sheet under her with perspiration, we thought it was a sign that she was getting better. But the second time it happened, we realized we had a problem. We were once again in Vianopolis, Brazil, where most New Tribes Mission missionary children attended school—only eighty or so miles from the hospital in Anápolis where Becky had been born. Now, Bob raced off to see if we could hire a car to drive us there immediately, while I sponge-bathed Becky, trying to get her fever down.

It was malaria, for sure, and there was concern we would not make it to the hospital in time.

We did, though, and the doctors bustled around. Becky was small by American standards but large by Brazilian standards, so she was given adult doses of medicine despite her age. This, in turn, affected her liver and turned her skin yellow and her urine the color of black coffee. I was told she had black-water fever, which was usually fatal.

Becky could hold nothing down, and she grew weaker and weaker. One day she whispered, "Please, Mumma, take me home. Even if I die, I don't want it to be here." So we returned to Vianopolis, where we were covered in prayer. I found my Merck's Medical Manual and followed it to a tee. She was to be given something to stop nausea, vitamin K as well as other choice vitamins, a tablespoon of oatmeal gruel every half-hour—I don't remember if they said that or if I added it on my own—and a daily bath and a daily walk. Most important was that she be kept happy and have lots of sunshine. This I could do.

We read, sewed, played with her dolls, and listened to music. Our sadness turned to joy as Rebecca slowly regained strength and lost her yellow glow. God is good.

* * * * *

God had many plans for Becky, and she became a soul-winner, a concert pianist, sang distinctly with an operatic voice, and became a schoolteacher. All these early years were simply a part of her preparation for life itself. I know you are proud of her, Mumma, just as I am, and I thank God for allowing me to be part of it.

Chapter VI

Tocantinia

$\mathcal{T}$he small, sleepy village of Tocantinia is in the middle of nowhere on the Tocantins River. Across the river lies Miracema do Norte, a little larger and only reachable by boat. Our town boasted of one small general store stocked with rice, beans, sugar, coffee, and a few choices of dress material bought by the meter. The town seamstress, Dona Darci, could look at a dress pictured in a Sears-Roebuck catalog and whip up an exact made-to-fit replica in two days. All the store needed to carry were needles, thread, and material.

There must have been a small gasoline generator tucked away somewhere in the back of the store, as every time someone in our village died, Schubert's "Ave Maria" would envelop the town with its sad, haunting melody, letting the people know. Death was close to all of us in this almost Godforsaken town. It was sort of like in Hemingway's "For Whom the Bell Tolls," with no one knowing who would be next to die, or how—when a poisonous snake or infected mosquito might bite, and our "Ave Maria" would play.

The closest time I knowingly came to having it played for me was when I had an allergic reaction to a vitamin B12 shot. Somehow, we had learned that low energy and listlessness could be eliminated by this miraculous injection. I had been weak for days, and when Bob gave me this injection, he didn't know I had anemia and would react. First, giant purple blotches started popping out on my body. I ran to Bob and said, "Look, these spots are coming on fast!" Right before his eyes, more blotches appeared. Bob yelled, "Run—you're allergic to me!"

It was many weeks before I could appreciate his joke.

My body itched all over and was swollen and discolored. We finally filled a tub full of warm water and added boxes of baking soda. Because I insisted on a tub bath and not a shower, Bob had brought up a tub from a town six hundred miles to the south. The fact that we had no running water did not faze me. There was plenty of water in the well, and large containers of it were kept full on the wood stove—we had to boil each day's supply of drinking water for twenty minutes. We did that at night and poured it into liter bottles to cool off for the next day.

Along with the tub, Bob had obtained a small refrigerator that ran on kerosene, so a few bottles of water were kept in there. Most of the space was needed for the meat, which we bought daily. In the wee hours of the early morning, a cow would be butchered, and someone from each household would go buy their portion. It was so fresh that when Bob came home and put it on the table, the muscles were still twitching. So now with the cold water to drink and a warm tub of baking soda water to sit in up to my chin, I had some relief. To keep me from drowning, one of the family members sat on the toilet seat across the room at all times.

Next, the reaction attacked my nerves, and I started crying like a drunken man gone beyond the happy stage of booze. Meanwhile, Bob was searching frantically through the large box of sample medicines which had been given to us by a pharmacist. He was reading to find out if anything could be used for someone with my symptoms. Finally, he came in triumphantly. In his hands was a jar of green salve. All the symptoms fit. Bob wrapped me in a towel and put me on a bed. I couldn't stand the touch of anything on my skin, so a clean sheet gently hid any personal parts; and then the green goo was put all over my body so that I resembled a child of the Jolly Green Giant. It really did help, though, and in time I settled down.

After a short sleep from sheer exhaustion, I woke to feel swelling inside my body. I felt it creeping up to my throat and knew that when it got higher, I would choke to death. Almost everyone in town came to check on me and brought food and any kind of pills they thought might help. "So-and-so had the same thing and this cured him," they would say. I thought, "Oh well, I'm dying anyway, so I can't do myself any worse harm." I took three pills out of each bottle, praying that one of them would really work. On the way back to my deathbed, I caught a glimpse of myself in a mirror and couldn't believe it. My face was puffed up, and the green stuff was blended into my skin. When Bob poked his head in a couple of minutes later, he asked, "Have you taken a turn for the worse? What's wrong?"

"I don't want to die," I wailed, "and have everyone see me looking like this!" God had mercy on me, though, and I survived.

* * * * *

Fear was not a stranger to me, and it took control of my life many times in Brazil—sometimes warranted and sometimes not. The first house we lived in had no window panes or shutters. While Bob was gone, the faces of two fierce looking aborigines appeared at the open window. They were friendly, but how was I to know?

The outside walls of the mud brick house did not go all the way to the roof, so as to allow for ventilation. Night after night, I was so overcome by fear that I couldn't sleep but kept vigil over my two sleeping girls, guarding against fierce-looking aborigines and bogymen. As years passed on, so did my fear level. Was I more accustomed to my situation, or was God answering my prayers for courage?

* * * * *

For some reason, lightning seemed always to strike in our tiny town. Two men had been struck rather close to our house, and Bob had run out in the rain to help. He applied CPR to one man, while people stood all around thinking that this American was crazy to be kissing a dead man. They had no idea what was going on but thought it was a miracle when the man coughed, puked, and sat up. This was not heard of before.

The second man, struck later, died.

One day when I was idly watching a torrential rain coming down, a bolt of lightning and a crack of thunder arrived almost simultaneously. I ran to the back door and saw a hen on its back, legs kicking in the air. What I saw next was like a full-blown nightmare.

Bob was coming across the yard carrying eleven-year-old Christina in his arms. She was limp and lifeless; and even today, in my mind's eye, I can see her arms hanging down lifelessly. God is gracious, and as Bob put her on the bed, she stirred and asked, "Where am I?" She had been hit by two balls of fire in the lower abdomen, and we were told later that because of the elastic in the waist of her underwear, the fire did not travel up her body. She was paralyzed from the waist down, though. Bob and I prayed aloud as we heated blankets and towels to wrap her with, and we massaged her legs and back over and over. When she first moved a leg on her own, we were all crying. We were alone—with God. He once again proved all-sufficient.

* * * * *

There were emergency situations in our little town, like the time a small boy was brought to our home. As was the custom of some children, he had wrapped a tiny bit of gunpowder in a rag to throw on the ground, where it would detonate like a firecracker. When attempting to close the tiny pouch, he wrapped a string around the top and tried to tighten it by holding one end with his teeth. When he pulled, the gunpowder exploded, blowing up in his face.

The dentist in our town had tried to sew up the gaping jaw and mouth, after which no one knew what more to do for him. Bob was not at home when the boy arrived. When Chris and I saw this gruesome sight, we decided to keep Becky away from him. She was put in her bedroom to play and sleep. Although

Chris was only thirteen, she took over, and we kept a helpless vigil all night — wiping the child's face, giving him drinks of water, and trying to soothe him. There was not much we could do, and the following day some people came to get him, hoping to take him across the river and put him on the mail plane. He died before they could make it.

* * * * *

Donna Margarida and Dona Beatriz were Brazilian Southern Baptist missionaries who not only opened the small—yet powerful—church in Tocantinia but also had a school built which embraced kindergarten through high school. These two stalwart souls had an interest in everyone, including Chris and Becky. How many times I have thanked God for the faithfulness of these ladies—they mentored as well as educated the children of the town.

Imagine my surprise when they showed up at my door for a little talk. This was long before my college days, but these two saints were there to tell me so early in my working life that they felt I had a gift for teaching and wanted me to teach kindergarten in their school. I found it funny. Me? Teach? That was odd enough, but to teach in Portuguese no less?

Hold on a minute, I thought—I was just beginning to hold my own in conversations with the adult women. But they were so adamant that I couldn't refuse, and so began my long nights of memorizing the nursery rhymes and songs in Portuguese. The children called me "Dona Elena." Betty was an unknown name in this country, so they used my middle name—Elaine. Dona is always just tossed in to be polite. Becky was five, and refusing to attend school, so we attended kindergarten together, where I learned the language alongside my daughter. Dona Margarida was a great boost to my learning her language, and I noticed she only corrected me when I made serious mistakes.

One day she corrected the pronunciation of a word spoken

by a kindergarten child who responded, "Oh no, that is the way my teacher, Dona Elena, says it." Dona Margarida and I decided these little ones might someday attend and graduate from high school, all speaking with an American accent.

*****

I tried so hard to teach my girls the Biblical ways. If someone hits them, I instructed, don't strike back—just turn the other cheek. My girls grabbed on to this philosophy with pleasure, putting their own interpretation to it...albeit from the aggressor's perspective—if one was lucky enough to get in the first jab, not only could her opponent not retaliate, but the attacker got in a second jab for free.

Both of my girls picked up Portuguese fairly quickly, and Chris took pride in her high grades. Becky, my shy one, ended up just studying at home with me. Before she even started speaking, she was humming and carrying tunes, letting me know she was gifted in music. But what does one do for a musical child in the jungles of Brazil?

Bob's mother, Vera Williams, had bought a portable pump organ when attending Moody Bible Institute and had somehow saved it all those years. Becky played it while visiting her grandmother in the States. The organ squeaked and groaned as the pedals were pumped, but Becky figured they were normal sounds, and she ignored them as she faithfully practiced out of her John Thompson Book. She learned quickly, and as I didn't play piano, it became harder and harder for me to keep even one lesson ahead of her—enough to teach. I had to do my practicing when she wasn't around. After all, who would respect a teacher who couldn't perform?

It was years before Becky learned I couldn't play the piano. Nonetheless, I have always been her most enthusiastic fan. In my little world, teaching became a big part of my life, and God raised a friend in the States to send both schoolbooks and music books for my two girls. No doubt I learned more than they did—except in music.

Becky continued learning music, and on each furlough in the States God provided excellent teachers and the wherewithal to pay for their services. It was easy to acknowledge that Becky had way outgrown the old organ, and once again Grandma Vera came to the rescue by donating money to buy a piano for her grandchild. Bob found a good buy in Southern Brazil and, after enclosing it in a wooden box, hoisted it onto the back of a Toyota pickup truck to start the thousand-mile journey. The farther north we went, the more curious people became, as they had never seen a piano before.

When it was finally situated in our home, people would gather outside as Becky practiced for hours on end. Finally, Dona Margarida decided it was time for Becky to give her first public performance and show that village some classical music! A few men rolled the piano out of our door and across the street to the Southern Baptist church, where fourteen-year-old Becky rose to the occasion, going from Debussy's "Clair du Lune" to selections by Mozart. The church was filled to capacity.

After the pews were filled, people lined the walls and filled the back area where it was standing room only. Outside, those tall enough peered through the windows and open doors while others stood around and listened. Where had all these people come from? The only advertising was by word of mouth.

Though our family has long been gone from Brazil, except for an occasional visit, the old piano remains in Tocantinia—perhaps waiting for its little owner to return.

Chapter VII

Babies Just Keep Coming

I remember the first baby I delivered on my own. The adventure began around one o'clock in the morning, with the moon shining so brightly that there was no need for a flashlight as I followed the man who had been sent to fetch me. A borrowed bed had been brought into the dimly lit room for the mother-to-be, as trying to give birth to a baby while lying in a hammock is a difficult, if not impossible, thing to do. A hammock was strung up for me to doze in if needed. It was.

Two so-called midwives were there, and the customary broth of black pepper, jalapenos, garlic, and onions had been given. I didn't think it would help, but I remembered going to a roundup in Texas where they lassoed the calves and gave each one a shot with a giant needle, branded them, and castrated them before turning them loose. I think they were so sore that it was hard to figure out where the most pain was coming from. This new mother would burn from her mouth, into her throat and into her tummy. Maybe she wouldn't even feel her labor pains.

I did, however, keep them from tying a rope around her stomach, which they believed would keep the baby going down where it should go without being able to come back up. I also did not allow them to stick a dirty finger down the mother's throat to induce vomiting, or to touch the mother or baby with filthy hands—they scrubbed, following my example. By six in the morning, we had a dear little girl.

* * * * *

I wasn't ready for my next birth. We had just moved from one house to another when the teenager from across the street came to the home. This was a foreign family and what I remember most was the woman's constant expression of "Oopla, oopla." I still use it. "Well," the teenage messenger, Claudia, said to me, "My mom is not feeling so well. She has a tummy ache." Upon further questioning, I discovered it was from labor pains, so I grabbed a pair of scissors, a bar of soap, some alcohol, and, as I could find no string, I cut down the mosquito net around the kids' bed and took the string that had been holding it up. Now prepared for jungle medicine, I ran to their house.

No one was home but the mother, and I found her in the bedroom, a large floppy middle-aged woman, lying in the birthing position and crying. "My baby is dead," she blubbered. "He died before he could come out." This was her third child, so she knew a little about birth. One glance showed me the head was halfway out, but her pains had stopped; and maybe it was a good thing. I soaped the appropriate area with good old Ivory bar soap and told her she couldn't wait for the urge, but had to push. As I guided the slippery little head, I could feel the cord around his neck. As I loosened it with my finger, we slipped him out; but he was blue and not breathing. I cleared his throat and then picked him up, holding him by his feet as I had seen in the movies, and slapped his little back.

It was a miracle when he started breathing. I didn't see him much after that—they went to the States. When the child was five, though, the family came back. He was a beautiful boy but spoiled like you wouldn't believe. The mother told me, "After that horrible spanking you gave him the day he was born, I vowed it was enough to last him a lifetime." Ah, well…

* * * * *

Perhaps my determination to learn how to deliver babies was part of fulfilling that purpose I'd set for myself, of saving children. On the other hand, just watching what happened to women in labor was enough to inspire any idiot to do something about it. Besides their limited resources, cleanliness was not incorporated or even thought about in the jungle villages. Water was often at a premium, so a good hand-scrub could be an inconvenience. When a bearing down pain presented itself, so did a person with a chair to sit on the mother's stomach so the baby wouldn't go back up but rather continue to head downwards towards freedom. Once arriving into this world, a poultice of cow manure was put on the baby's naval over the remains of the umbilical cord. This would harden and form a covering.

No one was allowed to mention how beautiful the baby was, or that could be a jinx, bringing about death. Those suspected of having an "evil eye" were kept far away. At the end of a week, many babies developed a fever and eventually died—of tetanus, no doubt, and likely brought on by the cow manure and not by a jinx or an evil eye. My thought was that if I did no more than allow the mothers to deliver in a clean and quiet atmosphere, with no one sitting on them or smearing their babies with manure, I would help both mothers and babies survive. I set up some rules which seemed a bit harsh to many, but they complied.

Rule number one was that the whole neighborhood was not to be allowed in the room, but only a couple of relatives. Also, screaming was to be kept to a bare minimum—they would need all their strength to get that baby out. I learned from a doctor who visited the village once a year how to keep the baby's head from bursting out, so I could take that life-saving measure of making sure the umbilical cord was not around the neck. I learned how, when the placenta would not break on its own after a long time in labor, to sterilize a hen feather with alcohol and reach as far inside as I could to puncture that tough little sac. Until that time, the only use of hen feathers I had heard of was for Ben Franklin to sign documents!

The day came when there was no other way but to apply this creative use of hen feathers for the first time. I was shaking and praying aloud as I shoved the feather where I had been told. A burst of water came forth and then, to my horror, a bloody plug. My deepest fears had surely come true—I had punctured the tiny head and now was holding a little brain in my hand. I jumped up screaming, "O meu Deus—meu Deus! Eu matei o nene!" Or "Oh my God—my God! I killed the baby!"

I put my head down and sobbed. Then a gentle hand touched my shoulder, and a quiet voice said, "Dona Elena, olha aqui," meaning "look here." It was Almerinda, my helper and my friend. She held out an object and there it was: a tiny baby with no hole in its head. I yelled, "It's a boy!" She told me to look again. In my excitement I had mistaken swollen labia for an appendage. It took me a long time to live down that mistake.

* * * * *

All my life I have been able to close out the world around me by inventing stories inside my head, even without televisions or books to inspire me. I could have kept Mary Higgins Clark in exciting plots for at least ten years! When I met Bob, he became my Prince Charming who rescued me from all evil. He filled my waking moments and my fantasy world. When he became unfaithful to me, it was not only a shock to my present world but killed any Prince Charming to me forever. He was no longer allowed into my fantasies, nor was any other man. My fantasies then concentrated on finding needy or abandoned children and rescuing them. Some of this fantasy world became reality as I reached out to help those I needed help from.

And there was Clovaci.

He looked like The Little Prince, with golden hair and blue eyes, and was as tiny and frail as a two-year-old could be. His mother stood there crying. Word must have reached her that I was a sucker for tears. He was dying, she said. He wouldn't eat and vomited constantly. We were five hundred miles from a doctor, and there were no means of transportation.

"What if he dies here?" I asked. "I wouldn't hold you responsible," she said. "Please try to save him." Here we go again,

Lord. I had no idea what to do. I tried though. We started with a bath, good food, vitamins, and much sleep. Because he wouldn't eat or drink, we pried his mouth open for a look inside. It was a mess of blisters and sores. I remembered when you, Mumma, had treated my mouth by making a paste of baking soda and water. Miracle of miracles, it worked on this little man the same as when you did it to me so long ago.

From the start, it was a battle of wills between Clovaci and me. Under other circumstances, I might have let him win more, but time was limited. He was a beautiful, lovable fighter. No doubt, that was what helped to keep him alive. He wasn't talking much yet, but with grunts and groans and jumbles, he definitely communicated. From a bedroom, where he was put for a nap in a hammock, he would make a sound like, "Nghuh!" I would echo back this noise from the kitchen. It was our game. We both pretended to be angry. I soon discovered that if I lay down beside him in the hammock, his little blond curls piled up on my shoulder, and he would go to sleep.

A short time before his arrival, I had been very sick with anemia. As a result, cooking healthy foods and getting lots of rest was working miracles on both of us—did God send this child to me because of his need, or because of mine?

Clovaci never rushed to greet me when I came home. He never kissed me hello or goodbye, but we were definitely bosom buddies. I really missed him when he left—healthy as he could be. If he missed me, he was careful not to show it. (Thank you, Lord, for sending someone to take care of me; I needed him!)

Then there were the twin baby girls who showed up uninvited. A woman, holding them both, stood in my doorway. The light of the fading day formed a silhouette from her lanky body. I invited her in, taking the two babies from her arms. I called for my two teenage helpers—Wanda and Maria Amelia. One took the babies, and the other rushed to make strong coffee.

"I hear you help people in need," the woman said. Her voice was just above a whisper. "I must go to the hospital right away.

Please take care of my two babies—and if you like, keep them."

I never did learn much about this lady and could not remember the names of the four-month-old girls. My Rebecca was six, and Christina was nine. They thought heaven had opened up and dropped two live dolls in our house. Becky claimed one, calling her Sonya, and Chris claimed the other, naming her Sandra, and so began the reign of confusion.

These two dear little girls had never had a diaper attached to them. It was like a marathon to capture them and pin a diaper on their small bodies. They kicked and flailed and screamed. Sometimes it took three adults, one to hold the legs, one to hold the torso, and one to arrange the diaper. These very poor babies were very spoiled babies. They had been allowed in only two places—someone's arms or someone's hammock. Suddenly their lifestyle, environment, and familiar faces vanished, to which they strongly and loudly objected. In desperation, I turned a table upside down—playpens were unheard of—pounded slats around the four sides, and padded the bottom. Voila!

I then put both diapered bottoms in it and let them scream it out. How glad I was that Bob was on a long trip to an aborigine village and was not around. At night, I hung a mosquito net from the ceiling, completely covering the playpen, now used for their bed. Soon they adjusted, and so did we.

I felt these two lively dolls needed more nourishment than just milk, so I added thin, well-cooked oatmeal to their diet. They absolutely hated it. One of my teenage helpers held the babies' noses and poured it down their throats. I also noticed that the babies cried a lot more around Wanda. Upon further investigation, I discovered she was pinching them, hard, when they would not cooperate—perhaps she was in training for becoming the lively teacher she became in later years. She came from a family of ten and was not too pleased with the new additions in my home, preferring it—and her work—the way it was.

The twins were with us until close to their first birthday.

Bob was noncommittal about them. His comment was, "Keep them if you want to." Perhaps I should have, but I felt the responsibility was too great for me alone, and I lacked the faith to trust God to provide care through me. After recuperating from surgery, the mother came by to check on them. She was so grateful to find them healthy and happy. Sadly we returned our twin girls who had been loaned to us for awhile.

Next came Eva.

Eva was a small Xerente aborigine girl who stayed with a Brazilian foster family close by. She had been with them on and off for quite some time, but when she turned eleven, she went back to her aborigine village because her mother had decided she was of marrying age—a marriage would mean one more man in the household to help with planting rice as well as hunting and fishing for food.

I happened to be traveling through Eva's village when I heard this awful screaming. (Maybe it was as the Apostle Paul said, "I, being in the way, the Lord led me.") I ran over to find the Brazilian foster mother on the outside of the thatch hut screaming, "You can't make her stay here. You can't! She has to finish school! She has to come with me!" The aborigine mother was screaming back, "She is my daughter! She is Xerente! She must follow the Xerente customs!" Eva?

Well she was wailing as loudly as she could, too. There was no one hiding emotions there in the middle of nowhere.

"What shall I do Lord?" I asked, but I forgot to wait for the answer. My words poured out. "Why don't you give her to me?" I yelled at all of them. Suddenly there was silence. "Eva, would you like to stay with me?" I called through the thatch. The women appeared, and there were nods of assent. I spoke to the aborigine mother directly, asking "Is it all right with you if she comes with me?" She nodded. Then I spoke directly to the Brazilian mother. "Is that okay?" Once again, approval. "Dear Lord," I addressed silently, "my big mouth and me! How come these things always happen to me?"

We took Eva with us to Tocantinia, which was five miles from the aborigine village. She was outfitted with Chris and Becky's clothes. Her favorite was a pair of jeans she inherited. She was a bundle of laughter and devotion. At first, we were afraid she would rob us blind and give everything we owned to the aborigines. But, to our knowledge, she never did. When we traveled from Tocantinia to Anapolis, she was just one of the girls and fit in as though she always had been with us. There was so much she had never been exposed to, especially when we took her to Southern Brazil—sleeping in a motel, life in a big city, etc. She loved all of it.

There is pain when I think of Eva now. Not for her, but for me. She was loyal and faithful to me and loved me dearly. There is no way an aborigine can leave Brazil. So, when I left Brazil to live once again in the United States, I left her behind in my home with my helper, Lydia. That was a loose end in my life that needs to be tied up, and I pray that God continues to bless her life—and finish the work He has begun in her.

Chapter VIII

A Place God Loves

*T*he cows freely roamed the streets in Tocantinia, as did the chickens and pigs. Dust filled the air as they plodded down the dirt roads. Children pushed pretend cars made from two wheels joined together with a rod, a walking stick tied onto the center of the rod—this allowed the owner to run and push his wheels at the same time, making hens fly out of the way, cackling as they went. Gnats, flies, and mosquitoes joined the menagerie.

People sat in front of their adobe houses, fanning themselves and greeting each passerby. I was just going to greet a little old lady when I glanced up the path in the wide field, which led to our little house overlooking the river. Bob was just heading home at the same time, on his Harley Davidson. A grazing bull was nearby and didn't like the sound or looks of that red motorcycle. He lowered his head, pawed the ground with his front hooves, and charged. When Bob saw him coming, he went even faster but hit a bump and flew up high in the air, turned a summersault, and landed. Then he jumped quickly to his feet and took off! The driverless motorcycle was right side up and still rolling, the bull was charging, and Bob was running for his life. Who needs television?

Bob enjoyed finding large tarantulas. At my first scream, he would come running with a bottle of rubbing alcohol and a match. When the hairy creature was doused, he would toss a lighted match at it, and the burning ball soon turned to ashes. Scorpions were different, sneaky little things, hiding in dark, damp locations. When a doctor told me that a tarantula bite or a scorpion bite would not kill me but only make me wish I would die, it took away some of my fear.

Now snakes did not fit into that same category at all.

On one occasion, Chris had been asked to step outside the

door and bring in a stick of wood for the stove—a demand, actually, more than a request. Everyone was tired from the trip we had just made from Pedro Alfonso to Tocantinia. All our belongings were stacked up in the back of a truck, and the men who had driven it were as hungry as we were. Oh, for a good old gas or electric stove to cook on…but the small brick stove with its wood fire would have to do. It was more like an open oven with a lid on the top to place the pans on. The heat mostly went up the chimney. There were only partial walls in the summer kitchen and therefore no need for windows or doors to close us in—it was more like a patio with a mud floor.

Chris came back in. "Mamai, there is no wood out there," she said. It was dusk, and I was irritated as I sent her back to the load of wood deposited by the door just a day before. On her third trip back to me, I grabbed her little hand and yanked her outside. "There," I declared and shone the flashlight on a red, yellow, and black highly poisonous coral snake, exactly where she would have mostly likely put her small hand on the woodpile. God had blinded her eyes—the wood was in plain sight.

This was just one of many snake encounters for my children. A few truly show God's goodness and loving care.

I was taking my two girls and a few teenagers about a mile away from Tocantinia to a cool, clean stream where the washing ladies often went to wash clothes. Dona Antonia and her two little girls were showing us the way; she laughed and talked, balancing a big bundle of clothes wrapped up in a white sheet on her head. She reminded me of Aunt Jemima on a pancake syrup bottle! The teenagers, Wanda and Concita, were running down the path with Chris right behind, trying to keep up with the group.

Suddenly, Wanda yelled, "Cobra!" as she took a flying leap over the long black snake crossing their path. Becky also jumped over it, but Chris was paralyzed. She couldn't see the snake and just said, "Where…where?" By the time I focused, it had raised its ugly head a good foot and a half in the air, and its wiggly

78

tongue flicked from its mouth. I was close enough to see it but too far away to help, so I fainted. But God was close enough to see it, close enough to help, and He didn't faint.

When we were still in Tocantinia, I went to answer a clap at the front door—the doors and windows were open, so there was nothing to knock on, and electric doorbells were out of the question. A hand clapping a few times was the way to announce, "Hey, I need to talk to you. May I come in?"

Dona Juanna, my neighbor, was standing there and started to talk to me about her pregnancy, asking if I would deliver her baby, when she stopped talking in the middle of a sentence and just pointed. I turned to see a small brown deadly poisonous snake on the floor of the room behind me. At that moment, Becky and her friend, Socorro, came out of a bedroom and headed in the direction of the snake. I screamed, "Snake! Snake!"

Becky stood still, but Socorro ran like mad and encountered the snake halfway across the red-painted cement floor—we washed and polished that floor daily, the teenagers pushing around the heavy polisher with Becky sitting on it to add weight while utterly enjoying the ride. So, when Socorro and the snake tangled, although we should not laugh at such a serious situation, it was quite a sight to behold—Socorro slipping and sliding, the snake similarly unable to gain traction on the highly waxed floor…it was utter confusion. It looked like they were dancing together.

Bob finally heard the commotion and came to save the day. The snake would probably have died of a heart attack had Bob not cut its head off with a machete first.

Chapter IX

Some of God's Creatures Join Us

Somehow our family accumulated many pets. There was Sophia, the tiny monkey with a halo of white fur on her head. She slept in a small hammock made just for her, which swung between the bedposts. Before she went to bed, she crawled into one of Bob's white socks and would not come out again until invited. She was like a small stuffed animal that had come to life. Then there was the rather large black and white owl that perched on our bedroom window sill and wisely watched all that was going on.

Another mischievous animal was a baby coatimundi. I realized he was cute and could fit into my hand, but I didn't know just how smart he was. One afternoon I decided to make a lemon meringue pie for supper. This little critter followed my every move and watched with much interest. Finally, the pie was done and looked like a picture out of Betty Crocker's cookbook. Putting it on a rather high shelf to cool while I went to shower seemed like a good idea, but when I came back out, there was little Coati just about to sample it. Somehow he had climbed onto a chair, then the table, and made a good high jump to the shelf. No doubt he had been planning that all along.

Another day, Becky found an armadillo and declared it was just the kind of a pet she had always wanted. The Brazilians called it a "tatu," and it suited this name. When Tatu ate, he slurped and smacked his lips so as to be heard all over the house. Thus, people with bad table manners were referred to as being like a tatu. The armadillo was more fun than the gigantic turtle that moved in, though they should probably both have been made into soup—both are very good tasting…and were not quite ideal as pets. We didn't eat them, but we did eat the tail of a caiman, a type of crocodile. When the aborigines brought it to us, they declared it was dead. Bob put it in a tub of water and touched its mouth with a stick. It is a good thing he didn't offer a finger.

Later two cute pets arrived around the same time and seemed to enjoy each other's company. There was the baby otter that could not see anything except what was directly in front of his nose. If I held his warm bottle of milk slightly higher than his face, he would have starved to death...but he really latched onto the bottle when it was held lower. His buddy was a baby ocelot, no larger than a kitten but with thick paws that he padded around on, quietly roaming around the house. Bob was his favorite person in the house, but he also romped and played with Otter, oblivious to the fact that the fur was all gone from the nape of his own neck where Otter had latched onto him and shaken him so often.

We always had an overabundance of parrots around our house...and parakeets. Parakeets make their nests on low ground, and it became that time of the year again when the tiny eggs were hatching. The Brazilian children were out snatching the little parakeets from their nests as they cracked out of their shells. It seemed to me that the whole town of Tocantinia was out to supply Christina with parakeets! That year she had eighteen bald, featherless ugly looking creatures given to her.

Their gullets were larger than their heads, and at least three times a day they all screamed for food. We made thin oatmeal gruel, opened their beaks, and poured it down their throats, which made their gullets blow up like balloons. I spent hours helping Chris feed those little things. As they grew, they were turned loose in the yard; and once there, they never again left. This meant we had tiny green birds in the lemon tree, the avocado tree, the papaya tree, the banana plants, and even the carambola tree.

Then there were the medium-sized parrots. One in particular just walked into the house and took over. He would not allow anyone to touch him and took it as his self-appointed job to just strut all around. Soon he became possessive of the family; and when a stranger came in, he would bite the back of their heel. Parrots don't just bite, though—they twist the mouthful they have, and it really hurts. Soon he became like a watchdog, and it is not considered a pretty sight to see grown men running down the street being chased by a parrot!

There were so many other pets we sheltered, but the large blue and yellow macaw stands out. When he was brought to us, his wings were clipped to prevent his taking off. His beauty could not make up for how loud and noisy he was, though—all day he shouted, "Arara, arara!" Perhaps that was the name of his girlfriend?

Bob did not care much for this creature, though he tried to be nice about it. One day he came to the bird perch and said, "Hey, look! Its wings have grown out again! I wonder if he can fly…" Bob stood on a chair, held onto the bird's wings, flapped them a few times, gave a gentle swoop upwards, and let go. My beautiful Arara flew high into the sky, looking even more beautiful against the golden sunset.

I went inside to rest and perhaps sulk a little after that. Now, to be sure, I am not scientifically minded, and every once in a while I wish I more fully understood some things. This is one: the bedroom had no ceilings. The walls went up to the tiled roof, so Bob and I had fashioned a ceiling out of old sheets by sewing them together. This, we reasoned, would be cooler than a true ceiling, while keeping rats and dust from dropping on us. This was a double protection as all beds had mosquito nets around them. On that one evening, I went in to lie down for a nap and closed the shutters to the high windows, leaving only a slit of light at the top.

As I settled down, I looked up at the ceiling, and there was a colored moving picture of all that was going on in the street outside my house. The sky was gentle blue, and the soft clouds floated above my head. There were some children playing in the street and people going into the church. I was fascinated and in awe. It was my own private colored television, with current events...and no commercials! I could watch what everyone outside my door was doing.

* * * * *

Tocantinia was busy compared to the aborigine villages. Here, there were dirt roads, and ours was the only vehicle in town. Bob had gone from motorcycle to jeep and later to a Cessna 140 airplane. He loved making roads and made one connecting Tocantinia with the two aborigine villages of Baixa Funda and Funil—around forty miles apart!

In Tocantinia we had a mud house, made by first framing in an area by crisscrossing small branches and filling it all in with a sort of red clay mud taken from the ground and covering it with a white lime when it was dry. Windows were just spaces left in the wall with crude wooden shutters that opened and closed. In each of the villages, Bob had made us a thatch hut similar to the aborigines'. Aborigines did not live in Tocantinia, and Brazilians did not go to aborigine villages except to inquire about a missing cow. The girls and I stayed in Tocantinia while Bob made contact with aborigines and prepared a house for us.

Having rested awhile in Tocantinia, it was time to pack up and go to one of the villages to spend three weeks. This meant bringing food that wouldn't spoil. I feel strongly that I invented granola. Oatmeal was an available, healthy staple, but it was not easy to find a place to cook it. The girls enjoyed making cookies out of raw oatmeal, powdered milk, and peanut butter, cans of which had been kindly sent by the U.S. to Brazil. But I wanted something easily obtainable. So I took the large iron skillet we had brought over with us on the boat, plopped into it whatever grease was to be found, brown sugar, and oatmeal. This I stirred and toasted until it looked done and packed it in the can it came out of. Then there would be oatmeal cookies. I was addicted at that time to feeding my kids hidden oatmeal and even added it to meatloaf and to gravy because I thought it was good for them—but not for me. After consuming so much as a young girl at the children's home, enough was enough for me!

Bob loaded the provisions, the two girls, and Princess, our German shepherd police dog, into the back of a tiny Toyota truck; he and I climbed into the only two seats, which were in the front, and we were all off to Funil, our favorite village. The aborigines warmly greeted us and presented us with a mallard duck with such perfect markings that it looked like a painted wooden decoy. The girls decided to take it for a swim in a little stream close by. I watched all three playing together, the duck being guided by a string around its leg. Then out of nowhere, an uninvited guest appeared and followed after the girls—they saw him, a poisonous snake, and screamed and splashed. This was not a good game to be participating in because the snake was catching up and he was determined to be the winner.

Chris, Becky and I screamed, but no sounds came from the snake or duck. In her hysteria, Chris dropped the string connected to the duck and, in so doing, helped the snake become the winner. Our last glimpse was of the snake following that duck silently downstream.

Oscar the Rat dropped from the eaves straight down with a plop. He was almost too ugly to exist—he had a long face like a miniature moose and bulging eyes. Without any fur, he was truly bare-naked. Chris and Becky brought him to me, saying "Look, Mama! He is so cute…and he is an orphan, you know. Can we keep him?"

In my previous encounters with rats, they were none too friendly. There was the night I couldn't sleep due to one of my frequent migraine headaches. I quietly climbed out of bed, away from the safety of a mosquito net. I went into the dispensary where the walls were lined with shelves holding rows of cans that had once held five gallons of gas but now held bolts, nuts, and other things Bob had put aside, as well as large covered containers filled with nonperishable food supplies. A cotton hand-woven hammock had been slung catty-corner across the room, and it was here I threw my hurting body.

The slow swinging of the hammock made a gentle breeze which soon rocked me to sleep…but not for long. I felt a plop on my chest and automatically reached up to grab the object responsible. It was soft, furry, and squiggly. As my hand went around it, I started screaming loudly and slung the thing across the room. Bob came running, gun in hand, as he was sure someone must have been murdering me. His adrenaline was pumping, so he didn't go back to bed until he found and shot the culprit. Usually, he was a pretty good shot—previously, he shot six out of eight bats hanging from the rafters; though, when we encountered five different deer while driving one day, he shot at and missed all five. So I wondered how he would fare with the rat…but his aim was true, and the rat was dead.

So when my girls brought me a rat like it was a pet…good grief! I had been setting traps for those things all my life! But I did what any mother would do to save face. I wrapped him gently in cotton batting and dipped a bit of the cotton into warm milk, and the little rascal latched on. Bob got in on the act and made a tiny screened-in cage, and we named him Oscar. We both got parent Brownie points from the girls but were rather relieved the day Oscar got strong enough to scamper off.

I told the girls right from the start, "Have as many pets as you want. Take care of them. Enjoy them; but if they die, run away, or get stolen, I don't want a lot of crying and carrying on. Enjoy what God gives you while you have it; and when it is gone, move on to the other things." They agreed and were really pretty good about it—like the time Becky's parakeet died.

Bob was not at home, but the three of us had a really neat funeral. We sang, prayed, and buried little Tweetie, who was a favored pet—but Becky didn't complain. A week later her father came home with much on his mind to share. In between his sharing, a quiet little voice said, "Daddy, my parakeet died." She repeated this a couple of times, and Bob would look up and say,

"I'm sorry honey," and go on with his conversation. We didn't notice when Becky slipped out, but I did look up when I got a whiff of a bad odor. Becky came marching in, holding the remains of the dead bird in her hands, and planted herself firmly in front of her father and said, "Look, Daddy. He's really dead." That time she received his full attention.

All the pets that landed in our home were one thing...but one day as I was baking a coffee cake, Socorro and Becky came in and presented me with a very tiny little girl. I was informed that the mother had given little Fatima to them to keep, and it must have been so because Fatima moved right in and made herself at home. This small girl was a chatterbox, for sure. Naturally, the girls left her with me all day, and Bob must have trained this midget because she followed me around, telling me how I should be doing things. Mostly, this was fine—I was used to it...but one day she really got to me. She told me how I should be plucking the feathers off the dead chicken I was preparing to cook. She pulled a chair up close so that she could oversee me better.

Her bossiness turned to anger when she saw me reach in to pull out the guts. In her mind, I was doing it from the wrong end—you were to reach under the breast, not through the rear end. I moved away and pulled her chair in closer and said, "You show me how, okay?" Wow, she dug her tiny hands right in and did a better job than I had been doing! I had a new appreciation for her after that, and that little one was in and out of our lives so much that she probably considered herself as having two families. What a little sweetheart God sent our way in Fatima.

Chapter X

The Good and the Bad Within us

*W*alking down the dusty path in the center of town when the sun was at its hottest, making it necessary to carry a small parasol for shade, my two girls and I were enjoying life when from out of nowhere a rock came whizzing through the air, hitting me in the head. Stunned, I looked around and saw two boys laughing. Without hesitation, and before my girls knew what had happened, I tossed the parasol down and shot off after one of the little guys. He looked so surprised and then took off running and finally ran into a house, through the living room, into the bedroom, and under the bed. I, too, went into the house, through the living room, into the bedroom, and under the bed. I dragged him out by one foot while his mother watched with a grin on her face. I don't think my talking phased him, but my chasing him gave him a real scare. His mother said that he never threw rocks at people again.

Bob and I believed in different methods for discipline. He defended his way by quoting Scriptures he had been taught. He spanked Christina with violence and declared that God's way to control a child was to break the will of the child and make them completely submissive. When I watch the life stories of religious cult leaders like Jim Jones and David Koresh, I can understand some of what went on there. Even I feared Bob's authority and had been taught that a wife should submit to her husband. My girls and I were not the only ones who feared Bob's authority.

One incident comes to mind when a young couple from Wycliffe Missions came to spend a few days with us. Bob came roaring into the house, furious because someone had allowed a roll of toilet paper to fall down the hole in the outhouse. Toilet paper was a rare commodity for us, and he threatened to spank both children if someone didn't speak up. Becky figured if she were going to get spanked anyway, she might as well spare her sister—her sister was her best friend. She owned up to a crime she didn't commit and accepted her spanking in full view of everyone.

Years later, the Wycliffe missionary admitted that she had done it but was too scared of Bob to speak up. She let a five-year-old take the blame and punishment for her. Becky likened it to Jesus taking punishment for us when he was on the cross, and she quoted this verse from the Bible, from John 15:13, "Greater love hath no man than this, that a man lay down his life for his friends." She didn't exactly lay down her life, but she accepted that punishment on others' behalf.

Bob had a real hang up about toilet paper. Because he didn't want to use the sandpaper-like paper of Brazil, he had someone send soft rolls from the United States. At one time, Bob held a family conference and told the three of us that we were to tear off three of the five-inch squares where it was perforated. Each of the three sheets was to be folded once and that was to give us three swipes. Oddly enough, this rule was enforced even when we were back in the States. Now, years later, one of my great pleasures in life is to wrap miles of toilet paper around my hand just to get rid of three drops. There are small ways to retaliate.

Bob never considered sanitary napkins a necessity—he didn't need them, so they were a waste of money. I was glad for the forty pairs of white socks Bob had. I couldn't put them in the garbage, but they burned rather nicely in the woodstove.

Often, what may seem strange is nothing more than an adaptation to some local circumstance—like repurposing socks or rationing disposable things we took for granted in the States. We lived very close to life and death and very close to the Earth, and in many ways this was marvelous. Neither Tocantinia nor aborigine villages had a need for garbage cans or garbage trucks. Any paper product one was fortunate enough to glean was used to start cooking fires. Leftover edibles, including peels and cores, were fed to hens, pigs, or any other livestock being raised for food. Tin cans were rare; but when one was found, the rough, ragged edges around the opened rim were hammered down to make a cup for drinking water. Vultures, known locally as urubus, devour any carcasses not eaten by people; and though I don't like to mention it, pigs eat excrement from humans and animals alike. Brazil has no garbage problems.

To Bob

Our hearts beat as one,
We fit—we belonged.
We had one goal,
We were as one—
        Or was it an illusion?

He was my man. He built
houses and septic tanks,
Repaired cars, sewed up
cuts and bruises.
He loved Harleys and trucks,
and I loved him—
        Or was it an illusion?

He taught the Scriptures to others,
and to his children.
He studied the word of God,
and I loved him—
        Or was it an illusion?

He never did quite fit in,
Bible school to the mission field.
He was often misunderstood,
but he was my man,
and I loved him—
        Or was it an illusion?

(Continued...)

He strove to find his
corner in life,
Loving God and striving
to please Him,
Sometimes going astray,
but always returning,
and I loved him.
  Or—was it an illusion?

- Betty Williams

Chapter XI

Of Snakes and Serpents

*L*iving in the aborigine village of Baixa Funda was never easy. One night we arrived at our thatch hut just as the sun was going down. We needed to light the kerosene lamps and get the hammocks strung up. Someone had tossed a dirty rag in the corner of the room. I gingerly picked it up by a small edge. The snake under it was not happy to be disturbed, and raised its head, ready to strike out. Having a fearless husband comes in handy. That snake's life was short-lived. I wondered if it was the same one that had climbed down the hammock rope of a fellow missionary, Günther, the previous night…

Günther had whispered a plea from the room next to us, and we went in stealthily with a lit candle. In the dim light we could see a snake slowly slithering down to where Günther lay in a regular hammock, one that lacked the mosquito netting. He did not move a muscle and hardly breathed. The snake went right on down the hammock rope and slithered over the whole length of Günther's body while we silently watched. I was glad for the jungle hammocks the girls and I had—there was a canvas cover, connected to mosquito netting that zipped closed, and also a false bottom prohibiting bugs from biting us through the fabric. The girls and I didn't have to worry about bugs and snakes while sleeping. Meanwhile, God, Who never sleeps, preserved Günther's life for the long road of service that lay ahead of him—the snake crawled out of the hammock and disappeared.

* * * * *

There were three young men sent up to the jungle area to work with us: Günther, Rinaldo, and Paulo. These young men came to us from Southern Brazil, where life is far more like it is back in the United States, meaning their adjustment to the jungle was as hard as ours had been. But we worked well as a team.

In spite of setbacks, work in the two Xerente aborigine villages pushed forward. When we first started to work with the Xerente tribe, they had no written language. They communicated with us and the Brazilians by speaking very limited Portuguese, while using the Xe language among themselves. We had studied linguistics; so, with the help of others, we started right away to put the Xe language into writing. When the first tiny primer was mimeographed and they began to learn to read in their own language, they were very proud—as were we all.

We were prepared to hear one of the Xerente aborigines— who called themselves the Aquain—share the Word of God in his native tongue. A few key Bible verses had been translated and now came the joy of seeing God work through this indigenous man; Günther had worked hard to prepare the man and organize the event.

Upon arriving, we sat on benches under a thatch roof. I was lost in the wonder of it all. Twenty-some aborigines, men, women, and children, were there. When it was time to begin, we all stood, sang a song, and listened to a Xerente prayer. Before I could open my eyes, a soft voice said, "Dona Helena, don't move. There is a poisonous snake under your bench." I swallowed my desire to scream while the man who warned me circled around behind me and killed our enemy. The ceremony continued, and Günther performed baptisms that day for the aborigines who had accepted Christ as their Savior, thus protecting them from serpents of another nature.

* * * * *

Sometimes a foreboding spirit fills the air so thickly that it is almost tangible. This was the spirit that greeted us in the small aborigine village of Funil. It was as though the four of us—Bob, Chris, Becky and I—were alone; even our quiet steps seemed to echo. No aborigines came out to surround us with welcoming chatter in what had so recently become a ghost town. We kept on walking, Bob in the lead with our two girls right behind him, and me following, very fearfully. The tribe at Funil was known to kill over very small provocations. Although we had tried to help them by showing them new ways to exist—such as cutting the end off of an empty five-gallon kerosene can and putting it on hot coals to create an oven to toast or bake flat yucca breads—who knew what dwelled in their hearts. What we interpreted as help could be misinterpreted as interference.

They had been the most unfriendly tribe from the start, but just a week ago they had sent a runner into Tocantinia asking us to please come and help—an epidemic of simple measles had broken out. These people had no immunity to childhood diseases brought in by outside contacts, and measles or mumps could wipe out their whole village, as indeed sometimes happened in the jungle. We had gone immediately; and with simple means and the grace of God, we nursed the people back to health. Most of them, anyway.

There was one teenager, Wakuke, who was almost beyond helping. She already looked like a skeleton with filthy paper-thin skin stretched over it. The Xerentes would never bathe, or even sponge-bathe, a sick person. This small girl, with bushy black hair matted together, was at death's door but had miraculously responded to prayer and medication. She sat up and smiled at us, motioning towards a gourd with sugar in it. She reached her bony, filthy fingers into the gourd, pulled out a few grains of sugar and licked them off her hand. She was weak, but her smile told us she was happy.

Now we were back from Tocantinia to medicate any remaining sick, check in on Wakuke, and celebrate. But no one was around. Finally, one frowning man stepped out of a hut. It was Caitano, the chief—a man for whom I had high respect.

He and his wife had taken in their granddaughter when both her parents died, and they doted on her and the young man she was planning to marry. There was amazing love and caring demonstrated in their family of four. Before meeting this man and his wife, I had not realized that the aborigines had such close family bonds and that love was as much a part of their culture as it was of ours. But that day, there was no pleasure in his face or in his voice. He flatly stated that Wakuke had died that morning. My thoughts ran rampant.

Would they blame us? Would they kill one or all of us? I hugged my five-year-old tightly on one side and my eight-year-old on the other and quietly prayed for all I was worth. He motioned us to follow him. I thought it might be better to make a mad dash for the jeep, but Bob followed him and so did I. We became aware of moaning and lamenting coming from a small thatch hut ahead of us. Getting closer, we could see figures barely outlined in the darkness of the small room. As we stepped in, we could see it was the frail and lifeless body of Wakuke, being held by a grieving mother. We could only express our sorrow; and as we left, the old chief explained that it was bad luck for any others to come out of their huts until the body was buried, lest the angel of death take one of them, too.

We were not allowed to stay while they performed the burial ritual. I did, however, see the grave that had been dug—it was like a skinny well, five feet deep and two feet in diameter. The young lady would be buried feet-first. I rather liked the idea; perhaps we should adopt this system in the United States, allowing room for many more bodies to be put to rest in our cemeteries.

* * * * *

When in the villages, our family often split up. Bob would go with the men while the girls and I stayed in our hut, choosing not to go with the women as they performed their chores, such as gleaning rice. My girls and I kept busy. Schoolbooks were like Mary's Little Lamb—everywhere we went, they followed us. Even time spent in the aborigine villages did not mean a vacation from lessons. After all, it was bad enough to be brought up in the jungle with a limited environment, but to also be illiterate and uneducated was completely unacceptable for my daughters. With this in mind, once breakfast was over and Bob left in a small canoe with some aborigine men to scrounge whatever food made itself available—fish, deer, or seasonal fruit—the girls and I settled down to the day's schoolwork. I taught them in a room shaped like a piece of pie, with a flimsy door that afforded us a small measure of privacy—which is unheard of in aborigine villages.

Bob was very creative and wanted to take a stab at making a round building, using thatch for the roof and to enclose our bedroom. Because there were no other real walls, animals used our home as a place of shelter when we were not there; horse's hoof prints and the footprints of many other creatures had made the ground almost like a red dirt sand pile, "inside" and out. Going against one of my own rules about never going barefoot in Brazil, one day found me shoeless as I taught the day's lessons. I enjoyed the feel of the cool dirt under my feet. Closed in our small classroom, away from the animals and the rest of the village, we heard someone clapping at our door. Leaving the girls to complete their written work, I stepped out.

I could not have been more surprised to find Santa Claus standing there. In front of me were ten big, well-muscled men, a machine gun in each one's hand…and each gun pointing right at me. I looked from one face to the other and followed my life's motto: "First you pray, and then you look for the humor in the situation," which was not hard to find. There we were, in the middle of nowhere, with no one around at the moment except the heavily-armed Brazilian soldiers pointing their machineguns at a barefoot teacher.

It was evident who was in command, because one man

carried his gun on his hip instead of in his hand. Perhaps he gave the orders of when to shoot... I walked up to him, extended my hand, and introduced myself. Still holding my hand in his firm grasp, the serious soldier asked me why I was smiling. My answer? "I weigh a hundred and three pounds, and any one of your giant men could throw me over his shoulder easily. Look—I'm even barefoot. I couldn't run if I wanted to."

With a sheepish look on his face, their commander gave an order for the guns to be lowered. After that, the men searched every little thing in the house. When they went into the pie-shaped section we used as a kitchen, their eyes lit up with the discovery of a one-burner kerosene stove and its portable Coleman oven on the top. The temperature gage on the outside made them feel that surely this was a short-wave radio. They'd spent days camped in the jungle, trying to locate such a radio, and there it was—we were spies after all, just as they suspected.

I still don't know what there was to spy on.

After cautiously opening the oven door and finding only warm cornbread, which I kindly offered to share, they were willing to sit and talk. By that time a runner—a child messenger from the village—had caught up with Bob and brought him back to the village.

The Captain relaxed and became friendlier. He explained that it was hard for the Brazilian government to understand why seemingly intelligent Americans would move six hundred miles away from civilization and other Americans to live primitively in the jungle. They thought that perhaps we were smuggling gold, diamonds, or other precious gems out of their country. The detail that really piqued their curiosity was that local Brazilian people—not the aborigines—told them we had a secret room in our small Tocantinia house...a room where no one but family members were allowed to go. Also, they said, we dug a large hole in our backyard and enclosed it on all sides with a four-foot mud brick wall, topped with a row of curved French tiles (which preserved the clay from the weather quite nicely).

Bob had arrived by then, and we stared at each other for a moment before the light dawned—they suspected that our classroom, a septic tank in the back yard, and an enclosed bathroom containing a flush toilet were integral parts of a smuggling operation.

The bathroom, at least, ultimately made sense to them. Outhouses were unsanitary and difficult to use, especially for little children. Local privies were not one- or two- or even three-seaters like the ones back in Maine when I was a little girl; rather, there was never any sitting at all in Brazil. Local outhouses just had a wooden or dirt floor with a circle cut out of the center and a deep hole under this opening. You go in, plant your feet firmly on either side of the circle, and squat, hoping for the best. Rinaldo's young daughter fell down the hole of such a privy one day, and her screams were heard far and wide.

Her mother, Gudrum, lay flat on her stomach, reaching down as far as she could into the dark, stinky hole as she yelled out, "Deborah, Deborah, give me your hand!" We were afraid her little one would drown in that foul mixture, but at the sound of her mother's voice, Deborah said "Okay, Mamma!" and stood up. After that, poor Deborah had five baths in a row.

To protect our children and make life better for ourselves, Bob decided to install a flush toilet inside the house—even though we had no running water. A septic tank was dug in the back yard; and as if by miracle, Bob knew just how to set up a septic tank—it seemed a miracle because he grew up in Chicago, not Maine. Where did he learn such things? A toilet was brought up from the south and installed in this "secret room" that only our family was allowed into. We flushed the toilet with water from washing or bathing.

As amazing as it was to see the native "place your feet and squat"–type outhouses, it was more amazing to see how the locals adapted to proper toilets. In a British hospital in one of the larger cities in Brazil, staff noticed that patients using the flush toilets were climbing up on the toilet, balancing their feet on the rim, and trying to adapt their method atop the porcelain bowl! The staff solved the problem by making flat porcelain toilets with grooved places to put your feet as you squat over a hole. When flushed, the whole square was washed with water. Ingenious.

* * * * *

We visited Baixa Funda frequently, including the time they sent for Bob to treat a child dying from malaria. Chloromycitin was a fairly new malaria drug, and each missionary kept one shot aside for family emergencies—but now ours would be sacrificed for an aborigine child. Bob brought a small thermos of warm oatmeal gruel and a soft flannel blanket to go along with the medicine. After treating her, the two of us returned to our thatch hut in the village, tired but happy that the sick one was showing a few new signs of life.

We had just dozed off when the child's father came in and announced that the witch doctor had arrived from another village to perform death rituals, saying the child would die within the hour. We stopped for nothing as we ran up the tangled path to the hut. The orange-gold from the dying embers of their cooking fire sent out an eerie light. Two forms were sitting cross-legged on woven mats, their brown bodies blending in with the dirty rags used as clothing. They rocked to and fro, their shiny black braids bobbing back and forth to the rhythm of their wailings in high falsetto. Their only accompaniment came from a few crickets; frogs contributed the bass with deep *ribbets*, and now and then an owl hooted in the distance, all contributing to a haunting melody of woe being offered up from this lonely spot in a remote jungle forest.

The witch doctor's chanting and dancing stopped as we came through the door. He stood over to one side with an angry scowl on his red and black painted face. A tiny, filthy form lay motionless on the floor in front of him. The dark and menacing eyes of the witch doctor met with the clear blue eyes of Bob. After a short stare-down, the witch doctor nodded and stepped back. Bob gently picked the child up, washed her face with a damp cloth, and declared that only God had power over death—and that wherever there is life, there is hope.

Then he prayed, his anger coming across. "Oh God, I can do no more than I have done, but these people need to see a miracle and see Your power at work—especially since this witch doctor has given up hope. Work a miracle, Dear God, and heal this child." All night he sat by her side and cared for her. The rays of the morning sun saw his faith rewarded as the girl stood up and asked for something more to eat. The witch doctor, overcome with defeat, slipped quietly out the door while the child's family rejoiced. God is still hanging around, ready to answer when we ask, even for a seemingly insignificant child in the middle of no-man's land.

Above: A recent photo of Betty's grandfather's store, which he built more than 100 years ago

Right: Grandma Vera, Bob's mother, with the "money tree" given on her 80th birthday. She lived to 100.

Below: The home in which Betty grew up. "So simple," she says, "but so surely home sweet home"

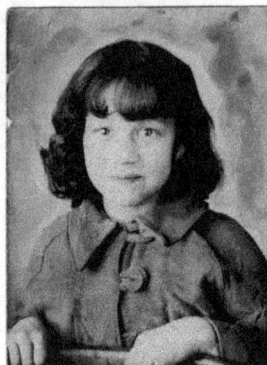

Top: Bob, Betty, Chris, and Becky, between trips to Brazil

Left: Betty, age 10, in the jacket Mumma made for her by tearing apart an old adult coat and turning it inside out

Middle: Betty, age 12. "Mumma said I had the freshest mouth in town!"

Right: Betty on her first furlough back to the US from missionary work

Above: Leaving Vianópolis for the 600 mile drive to Tocantinia. Betty and the girls rode on top, hiding under a tarp during a thunderstorm; lightning struck one of the bicycles.

Below: Goods and people cross the Tocantins River by ferry boat

Above: Betty and Becky washing the day's dishes in a creek near Baixa Funda

Left: A village girl winnows rice; wind carries away the chaff

Below: The proud chief of Baixa Funda

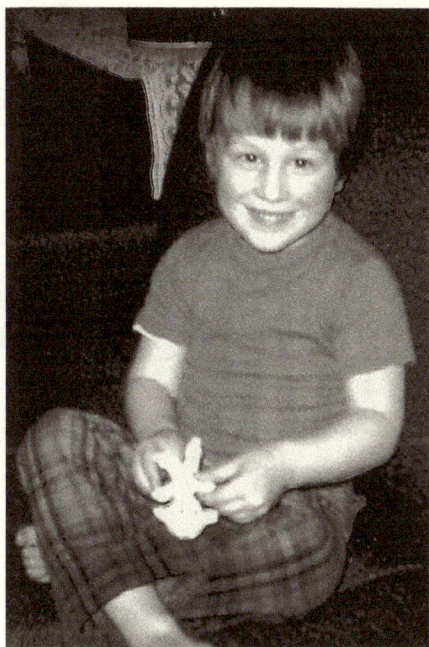

Above: Michael, nearly age 4 and happy to have joined the family

Right: Betty as a toddler

Below: Kind chief of Funnil Village

MOMMY

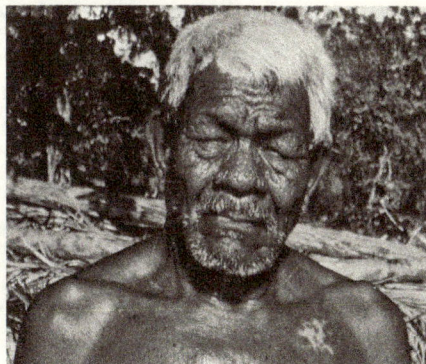

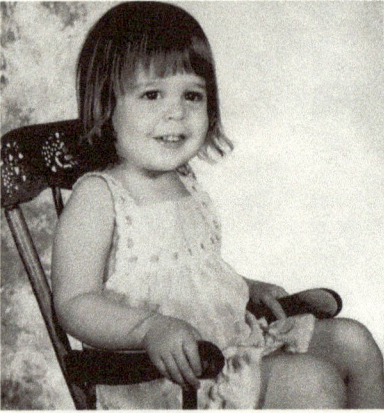

Above: Sri, shortly after entering the family

Upper Left: Sri Dhyana returns from her service in Iraq

Left: Sri and Michael, dressed for a tap dance routine

Below: Michael trained police dogs, frequently involving the whole family

To Mother

Thank you for the love
The hugs, the kisses, the lullabies.
Thank you for the typing
And the two years of college.
Thanks for letting me polish
The red cement floors until they shone like glass
And for letting me chop wood and kill chickens
And then serve them with rice.
And for little white lambs and fluffy yellow baby ducks and
    chickens.

Thank you for the poems—
Like: "I'm hiding, I'm hiding and no one knows where"
And "Gee up an bar the door!"
And for stories; Jungle Boy and Tom Sawyer and Heidi.
And for the long curls—
And also for the short bobs.
And for trips to sparkling streams
And fresh donuts after school.
And for the hours of listening
While I sat on the kitchen step.
And for letting me adopt other "Moms" whenever I felt
    the need,
And for suffering on through with me, the years of turmoil
    I endured.

(Continued...)

And for the early years of strong morals and strong faith
and total honesty.
And for perseverance
And for the fairies in the woods and for the elves behind
the rocks.
And for loving my baby,
Having worked out the "bugs."
And raising her like me…only if possible—better—having
the advantage of hindsight.
I saw you clearly in my dreams last night—as you were at
30
—As I am now. You too at 30 looked 20—as I do now. It
was so much fun having a real pal then.

- **Christina Williams**

Chapter XII

A Life Beyond

*I*t must be wonderful to always know exactly which decisions to make in life. The Bible gives some guidelines, but often there are two or three good choices that could be made. So it was with our little family of four. Chris was in the States, attending college. Our family had never been that separated for so long a time. Becky would be going into her last year of high school, either in Brazil if we stayed or the US if we returned. We decided, right or wrong, to leave our friends and ministry in Brazil and return to the States for awhile. Life moved fast and was good for a while but then deteriorated quickly.

We spent our first year in Wisconsin, where Bob studied for and received his aircraft mechanic license; Becky took music lessons and finished high school; and I remained true to my calling as a teacher of children by working as the well-paid director of a new daycare center. When I left the States twenty years earlier—shortly after World War II—the Head Start programs and daycares were non-existent. This industry was new to America and certainly to me. I was going to apply to the program as a teacher, but I figured that they could always lower me to a teacher…but would never just raise me to a director. So since that position was open, too, why not aim high?

When they actually hired me as the new director, I panicked. What does a daycare center do? How is one run? How does a person manage so many children? I received the good news while visiting family in Maine, so my drive back to Wisconsin included many stops to visit daycare centers all along the way. One of my mottos has always been, "Get the job first; *then* train for it." I had some catching up to do, and with God's grace, it worked out. Only three children were enrolled when I started, but there were fifty-two before the year ended.

That was a profitable year, aside from how Chris was growing away from us—or had already grown away from us. One of the reasons my heart let her go to the States a year ahead of us was because of her constant battles with her father. Should I have gone with her? The family we sent her to stay with while she studied seemed made-to-order, but life became harder than ever for Chris. Stupid things took place, like being forced to eat a large boiled potato at almost every dinner. She was gaining weight and had little control over it. It was hard to stay in touch across the great distance between us, especially with so much of our time spent in the jungle. She and I had been so close, but now she was alone. Were I to do it over, I would not have let her go into the world alone like that.

But she had to get away.

Chris had come to me in Brazil and told me how her father had improperly kissed her. When confronted, Bob strongly denied it, but the two of them grew apart. Chris carried memories like that about her father as scars all her life, feeling frustrated, alone, and helpless.

The space between Christina and her father grew larger and drove them farther apart through her college years. Then she informed us that she wanted to marry a man we had never met, which bothered us greatly; that he was black fed into our uncertainties. We so wanted her to wait, finish college, and lead a fulfilled life. When we showed strong disapproval, Chris broke with her family ties and pulled farther and farther away. Her husband-to-be called me on the phone and informed me that I would be dead before morning—he said a group of his friends were joining him in an all-night prayer vigil to call God's wrath down on me in the form of a horrible death, and I would soon have earthworms in my belly.

Bob had taken a construction job in Chicago and had gone ahead without us. Becky was attending a small college in Pennsylvania but was planning on going to the American Conservatory of Music in Chicago, so she and I were packing her up for the move. We did not get much sleep that night but prayed much for Chris and our own safety. We were in a small apartment close to the college. Although we pleaded for God's protection, we spent a very fearful night, not knowing what more their threats might involve. After her marriage, Christina and I grew apart rapidly and remained so for many years.

* * * * *

Eventually we moved to Maine, where Bob's mother Vera had bought a small cabin for me so that I would always have a place close to the home I loved. She and I were very close, as she lived with our little family for many years.

In Maine, I found a ready-made job at Head Start. Wisconsin was my training center, so now I could teach four-year-olds much easier, while going back to college to complete my teaching degree. I stayed three years, while Bob repaired and added on to our small house. He put in a bedroom with a bath attached. As he refused to work outside the home—which was very out of character for him—it was a mystery to me how he bought fancy tools and building materials…and how he planned to help provide for our family once he was finished with his projects.

Alas, he had a secret plan for the room and also for making money. He took his uncle Bob out of a nursing home and moved him into the private room and bath when it was completed. Along with Uncle Bob came a large monthly retirement check and many stocks and bonds. It was a long time before I realized what my Bob was up to. He had practiced for hours until he could copy Uncle Bob's signature; and over time, all of the stocks and bonds were cashed and the money was deposited in a secret account in only my Bob's name. He left paranoid Uncle Bob as my responsibility, and nothing in my life previously had prepared me for that—this bent-over, gray-haired old man woke up cursing and yelling obscenities, carrying on all day and not relenting until his sleeping pill kicked in at night.

Being completely out of his mind, Uncle Bob could not carry on a coherent conversation. Not only was his mouth out of control, but all of his bodily functions were as well. Urine and feces coated his room. Just walking into our house could cause uncontrollable vomiting. Needless to say, we stopped inviting friends over, and those who used to just stop by for a cup of coffee quit coming.

After a year or so, with close to one hundred thousand dollars hidden in his secret account, my Bob found a quiet place to lodge Uncle Bob for a third of the pension he received... and there he stayed until he passed away, at which time we missed the two-thirds of his pension we had been living on. Bob felt completely justified. How can Christian men ever be so dishonest and feel so justified in doing such horrid things?

* * * * *

Amid that turmoil, Becky started college at age sixteen. Being brought up with aborigines in the jungles of Brazil was not conducive to blending into college life, and she planned to live at home, which meant she needed to commute. My salvation was at hand. I could get away from the two Bobs and help Becky at the same time; our forty-mile daily trips to campus brought us even closer. When she felt too shy to attend class, I would go with her and audit, giving us more to talk about on our trip home.

Sitting in those classes was like putting a healthy feast before a starving woman. I couldn't get enough. Soon I was signing up to take courses for myself and loving it. At that time, there were not many older students in classes—and certainly not many my age—which motivated me to push even harder to finish so as to get on with teaching and helping children, my heart's true desires.

Just walking into a school building made me feel right at

home—I was where I needed to be. Criticism came flying at me from many directions, with people saying things like, "You will be close to fifty before you graduate. No one will hire an old lady!" But God had plans for me. I did rush it a bit, taking seven courses one semester—twenty-one credits, or six more than the norm. In one of my summer classes, there were several teachers and a school principal getting recertified. We carpooled, and on our long rides home, I began reciting what we had learned from the professor, presenting it in my own style and twisting things my way.

At first, the principal thought he must be hearing things, but then he caught on and laughed heartily all the way home. The more he laughed, the funnier I became. All my life I had been told I would be either a performer or a missionary—maybe my life would be long enough to do both.

This principal took me under his wing and guided me into the school system by pushing, coaxing, and prodding me each step of the way. I thank God for Mr. Savage. I graduated in June and, with his help, started teaching in September. At last I was doing what I had been born to do—teach!

* * * * *

Bob had me completely snowed under. I was of little value except for marital bliss and to make sure that the house was clean and that his three meals a day were cooked the way he wanted them and served on time. Bob never hit me, but ruled with negativity and words. There was only one way things could be accomplished—Bob's way. Because I was living in submission, as I deemed right, I really felt Bob's way must be God's way.

Sunday mornings brought a herculean challenge to the Williams' household—specifically, to me. There were the two children to bathe, dress, and feed; freshly washed clothes to be ironed for Bob, and breakfast that needed to be on the table in time…and God forbid there should ever be dirty dishes left in the sink. There was no division of labor—I was the labor force. Why was there such a fight to free the slaves while wives still lived under bondage?

For me, even offering a comment or opinion while conversing with others was forbidden. Aside from my open relationship with God, I felt like an empty shell, or robot, striving to please my earthly master. I wondered how many other Sunday homes were like ours. Was it hypocritical to smile at others while stinging so badly inside? What does a person do?

I remember a time when, after Becky was born with so many medical problems, we decided to see what faith healing was all about. Friends took us to a Kathryn Kuhlman meeting, where it was said that miracles took place. After the sermon, Kathryn Kuhlman came right up to Bob and spoke a few words to him, to which he responded. Then she firmly placed her two hands on his shoulders and prayed in a loud voice, "God, show this man the true way of salvation and save his soul." The ride home was a quiet one, but each of us wondered *is this truly an ungodly man in this car, or is this just the idiosyncrasy of a faith healer?*

Bob opted for the latter, but I wondered; if it acts like a duck and quacks like a duck, well... But, how could an ungodly man expound the Bible and have such lasting responses to it? Was it a matter of God blessing His Holy Word no matter who was uttering it?

I don't wonder anymore, but I do keep my conclusion to myself.

* * * * *

My older brother always called me a smart a**, and my teachers always said I was not living up to my potential...but until I went to college and graduated, I didn't recognize the implications of what they had observed.

Things at home were going from bad to worse. Becky, having graduated from college, had her own apartment and was going through her first year of teaching. Chris was still removed from our lives. But there was a new female in the Williams household.

Kerry was the age of my own daughters and was a pretty, sultry redhead. She had five boys and one girl of her own already. Every afternoon when I came home from work, she would be parked on my steps. We would all go inside where she would sit, smoke, and drink coffee while I puttered around making supper for everyone. What were her children doing? Anything they wanted to do. Sometimes the toddler would mess on the floor and walk through it and around the house. There it would stay, unless I cleaned it. If the baby's diaper was messy, I changed it. This went on for months. The hard part was not Kerry and her kids; the hard part was the flirtation going on between her and my husband. She would come in wearing white shorts, with her face all made up; and from the time he came in to supper, they would sit and visit into the wee hours of the morning.

I had to go to work every day, so I would throw a mattress on the living room floor to put her kids on, and I'd go to bed while the two of them kindled their flame. One morning, around three, I came down the stairs and asked if Bob would like me to drop Kerry off at her house. She had left the children home that night, and they had been talking or whatever for hours. He finally took her home…at five. He returned from the five-minute drive to her place an hour later.

It was all in the name of religion, of course; he was having a ministry with her, he said…their relationship was not hidden, after all, and they had nothing to hide, he said. Some evenings they would go off to some affair together, and I would stay behind, babysitting her children in my own home. I prayed, "Lord, you told me to be a good wife, didn't you?"

One day, Kerry's car wouldn't start while she was far from home. We had to drive quite a way to get to her. Bob got the car started, and then he and Kerry drove home in it together, while I drove our car home alone.

I felt a wall closing in around me. Rebecca was homesick

for Brazil, so together we saved enough money to make a three-week trip. I felt I would lose my sanity if I stayed and watched Bob and Kerry any longer. The agony was tearing me apart.

Michael

Not flesh of my flesh,
Nor bone of my bone.
But still, so miraculously my own.
Don't forget for a single minute
You weren't born under my heart
But *in* it.

- Betty Williams

Chapter XIII

Mike Makes It

A week before we were to leave for Brazil, Kerry brought her three-year-old boy to me. "Betty," she said, "I want you to have him. See his neck?" She showed me two deep bruises on his neck. "I almost killed him." She was crying. "I'm afraid that someday I will. Later, when he asks, tell him I gave him away out of love. I hate his father, and I'm afraid I'll take it out on him."

"Look," I said, "I'm not playing games with this kid's life. If you give him up, it's for keeps."

"It is for keeps," she said. She kept her word.

We got legal custody right away, so Becky and I could take Mike to Brazil with us and adopt him when we returned.

Now, if I had walked into an adoption agency and picked a child out of a lineup, Mike is not the one I would have chosen. On the other hand, he was handpicked by God just for me. We were heart-united from day one. I had said to a mother of five boys, "I have only raised girls, never a boy. What shall I do?" She didn't hesitate a minute before replying, "Just keep a good sense of humor…" It was some of the best advice I'd ever had… and was already second nature to me. And now, here we were in Brazil.

After getting off the plane, we had to take a bus to our next destination. The bus depot was built on an overpass where busses drove up to unload and reload passengers. The ramp off the highway was for busses only, or for vehicles bringing or picking up passengers. We had been dropped off by an airport shuttle bus and had gone directly into the terminal. Until going outside the depot, we didn't know of any danger…but Michael had spotted it right away and was drawn to it, running towards the edge of the unfenced overpass where far below us cars were whizzing at high speeds. He walked as close as he could to the edge and thumbed his nose at the cars one hundred feet below. The metal strip on which he walked was five inches wide.

I spoke softly so as not to startle him and make him lose his balance. Very quietly, I said, "Come here, Honey. I have something nice for you." This was not what I wanted to yell out at all. This was a learning experience for me because I discovered it was the Brazilian way not to over-protect children.

* * * * *

Pão de Açúcar (Sugarloaf Mountain) has a very high peak, where the view is beautiful as it looks over Copacabana Beach… but there were no precautions taken to prevent children from toppling over the steep incline. Also, there were no such provisions at the famous Christo Redentor (Christ our Redeemer) statue, which was so high up on Corcovado Mountain that the view was like looking down from an airplane. I enjoyed the views from the mountaintops, but kept a firm hand on the children.

Mike loved being up so high. This was Mike's life: in a fancy restaurant at the airport in Rio de Janeiro, he made a waitress come running when he shimmied up a high metal pole to place a handprint on the ceiling. Later, back in Maine, he rode his sled down through a path in the woods that was overgrown with giant pine trees, lying the whole time on his back and watching the clouds in the sky and trusting that he would be all right. He told me years later of how, just before coming to me, he had wondered if matches burned cloth. In the small apartment where he lived, he touched a flame to the kitchen curtains and couldn't believe how fast the flame grew and engulfed the wall. He got his two little brothers out of the apartment and then pounded on a neighbor's door and convinced them to call the fire department; his mother had just left for a short errand to the store. All that, and Mike was only three. *No Fear* was and is his motto.

Mike and I had an instant connection. We touched, loved, understood, and reached out to each other. I was amazed at this tiny human being thrust into my life, and we were united in our hearts from day one. Then there I was in Brazil, with my daredevil, my loveable three-year-old boy, who loved everything and everyone.

While in Brazil, we visited my sister Mary and her husband Lawrence, also missionaries. Mike was confused because he was surrounded by three women with similar traits—Rebecca, Mary, and me. He would walk up to my sister and ask her, "Are you my mother?" Tears would stream from her eyes. She'd say, "No honey, I'm not. But I love you, too." They would stretch out their arms for loving hugs. Since then he has never had any doubts— he was mine, and he always knew it.

* * * * *

While in Brazil, I was learning a lesson. Being five thousand miles away from Bob didn't ease my pain; it only increased it. Bob's letters were full of stories of what he and Kerry were doing—where they were eating out, their cute experiences together, and so on. Did he think that sharing such things with me made them all right to do? He was the one who told me how his father took these same appalling actions many years ago, bringing a girlfriend into his home and telling his wife she was to bear with him until the infatuation wore itself out. Further, she was not to share her hurt with anyone because it would ruin his ministry as an evangelistic singer. Behavior modeling is the best teaching device any parent has, and Bob learned well from his father.

Our friends became concerned. When watchdog Betty was close by, they figured I could keep Bob in line…but with me gone, they took time to write to me clear down in Brazil to tell me of their concerns. "You must come home to take 'care' of Bob," one friend wrote.

I thought, though, "He's yours, Lord. You take care of him. You be his conscience. You show him right from wrong." The load was getting too heavy for me to carry.

Chapter XIV

I Believe I Can Fly

*I*t was my forty-ninth birthday, and my life seemed at an end. I was alone in a shack with no water, no electricity…and no food! Well, not really alone—four-year-old Mike was with me, and just as hungry as I was. Perhaps he was an angel in disguise, the keeper of my sanity. Becky also joined us.

Just two months before, we had been elated—I had finally graduated from college. During the outdoor graduation ceremony, a man dropped his wallet on the ground under the bleachers; and Michael scrambled after it, eager to help. With his three dollar reward, he treated me to a hot fudge sundae on the way home, proudly sitting with my cap and tassel on his head. Oh, what a celebration!

Later that week, adult education was in the news, and cameras rolled as I posed on the Capitol steps in Augusta while being interviewed about going to college at such an advanced age…and graduating. My twenty-four-year-old daughter, Becky, watched with proud tears streaming down her face! I had my picture taken with former Maine governor Edmund Muskie and had a lovely talk with former governor Kenneth Curtis. I fell in love with politicians.

And now, here I was leaving a twenty-eight-year marriage, and all was desolate. Bob and I had lived separately for long periods of time for various reasons. My daughters and I stayed in Tocantinia quite often while Bob was in one of the aborigine villages or traveling to attend a conference or taking care of some business matters. While in the States, we would often be in different locations for one reason or another…but this was different. It was a change I had been considering for a long time. One morning I gave myself a good talking to, saying, "Betty, either shut up and take it, or get out once and for all." I decided it was time to leave.

The cabin that Bob's mother reserved for me had been in her name as well as mine, but this angered Bob; and he had worn her down until she took her name off the paperwork and put his on instead. What she tried to keep from happening, eventually took place, and Bob took over. After the divorce, Michael and I had nowhere to stay.

Whenever I drive by that little place, I think "That is *mine*. How could you have taken that, too, away from me, Bob?" Bitterness and resentment must be siblings—identical twins, perhaps.

For the first time, I felt guilt. I had not felt guilt since I was ten years old and my brother stole a package of gum from my grandfather's store and shared a piece with me—after that, I had nightmares of police in full uniform grabbing me out of bed. Right then and there, I had decided that nothing in the world was worth the mental torture. I did many mischievous things, to be sure…but with no self-recriminations. That was the change. In time I thought my conscience was dead, because nothing seemed to bother me. But, if it died, it was now resurrected. Guilt about the divorce, and all it implied, wrapped itself around me like a heavy, stifling blanket.

From the start, my marriage had been iffy. When my mother saw Bob sitting in our clunker car, steering while I pushed it to get it going, she felt right then and there that that was indicative of what my life would be if I married the boy. But, as I had been allowed to make my own decisions for years, that decision, too, was mine to make. Bob had decided we should leave college to join New Tribes Mission…which I had never heard of. In fact, I had never been out of New England and was quite naïve as to what lay in store for me. Bob had not even graduated from high school; but his pastor, Lance Latham, had been a college roommate with the dean of our little college and pulled some strings—which proves again that it is often not what you know, but who you know.

All of that was long ago. Now I was alone in the little cabin, scared and hungry. Bob said I created my own problem, so he didn't care if I ate or not. I had quit my job, in hopes of being accepted as a teacher in a public school in the fall. I wondered, "Where are these church people I have lived with, loved, and served for so many years?" When I decided to get a divorce, I dropped out of the church so I wouldn't accidentally bad-mouth Bob, as I figured he needed the security…and not one friend came by to see me or help me.

But that was my home church. I began my Christian walk there. I grew up there. I was loved; I was known. No one but family came by my cabin. This should have prepared me for what was to come…

To make ends meet, I taught school during both days and evenings, and I also became a weekend mother to six disturbed teenagers. Mike and I would go to the group home on Friday nights and leave on Sunday nights. Before long, I received an official letter from the small Baptist Church in Marston's Corner, the one that I had loved so dearly, informing me that I had been dropped from the church membership due to lack of church attendance. No one ever called to ask me why I wasn't there, or if I needed anything. Was it because I had filed for divorce? What had happened to love and understanding?

* * * * *

Bob's many flirtations began right away after our marriage. They went anywhere from eye contact with a girl to having arms wrapped around each other, which might have been innocent enough perhaps if not for the kissing and hugging as well— then it all seemed deceitful. These were things I saw. I don't know how far it went, when I couldn't see what was going on. And there we were, training to be missionaries!

I was being taught that a wife was to be submissive in all things and even be a doormat if that is what my husband decided to use me for. Down through the years, help was available, but I didn't know how to make use of it and still keep my marriage. I decided it was my personal cross to bear; after all, didn't everyone have one? I turned my surroundings off and drew into a close personal relationship with God. I would get down on my knees with the Bible opened in front of me.

The book I read most was Hebrews. I mulled and prayed over each verse until I felt I had touched God, or He had touched me. It was like climbing Jacob's ladder, hanging on to the angel for dear life until a blessing came. Jacob was left maimed after the struggle and would always limp, token-blessed.

I had learned from being alone so often in Brazil that when I felt inner unrest, but didn't know why, I could always depend on God. I would fall to my knees and pray over every situation and person I knew. When the deep-felt source of anxiety was reached, I would recognize what my problem was because there would be a flood of tears. Having a psychiatrist around might have been a help, but my way worked, too. I always wondered, *what would I do in such-and-such a situation?* I sought solace from my anxiety, while making plans I would probably never have the courage to follow. If certain things were to happen, I worried…what would I actually do about them? But God is kind and gracious. Perhaps having an emergency plan of action was counter to living by faith, but it has always been a need in my life.

* * * * *

I started teaching in September and got a divorce in November, with no one in the school the wiser. Once again, I was hired first and filled in the missing educational courses afterwards. My major in college had been in psychology, but my position was as a remedial reading and math teacher.

Starting over so late in life meant that I needed to live "full speed ahead." I taught in day school, plus night school, then added weekend teaching, too. The money helped, but was never my complete motivation. I would have done it had I been a millionaire.

* * * * *

Reading! I loved to read, and I loved to teach others to read. As a child, when the lights were turned off and it was time for me to sleep, I read by flashlight under the blankets to finish my books. My best friend Alice and I were so excited over reading and discovering new stories that we learned to save time by each reading a novel and then sharing what we had read by having a sleepover. Heaven help the one who left out any pertinent details of the book we had read, should those details later be discovered. Alice's mother was our teacher and supplied us with books as fast as we could devour them.

In the summer of 1978, I sought work at a Christian camp in Rumney, New Hampshire, in order to pay for Mike's camp expenses. For me, this meant working in the kitchen from seven in the morning until six thirty, with two hours off. In addition, I was expected to attend all evening services from seven to nine thirty. For this, I received Mike's camp expenses, my room and board, and twenty-five dollars a week. There must have been a better way, had I taken time to find it.

While this meager sum covered our expenses and I enjoyed the people, a restless spirit was within me; and I felt strongly that one of my loved ones was in need. Thus, I spent much time in prayer.

Christina was having her fifth baby, which she had decided to give to unmarried Rebecca. One critical problem was that Rebecca was in Brazil. She had found work in a university, but was suffering from culture shock. Her main symptom was screaming loudly in her sleep. Even though making phone calls across the ocean was an expensive and complicated task at that time, Becky's friend Socorro called me on the phone and said I needed to get Becky home.

When I learned of Christina's pregnancy and her plan to give the baby to Rebecca, I learned also that the baby was in the wrong position and could make birthing more difficult. I felt as though I was in an unreal world and the floodwaters of my dreams were getting higher. I felt I must do something.

I talked it over with Mike, and we decided to leave camp and head out for Southern Illinois to help Chris. When I got there, the heat was sweltering. Chris loaned me a pretty cotton sundress, and we walked a lot. She didn't want me to stay for the birth of the baby, though, and I felt rejected and hurt. Some of her close friends were to attend in my place.

"Lord, heal my wounded spirit," I prayed. "Calm my unrest and show me my next step." With nothing better to do, I headed back to Maine. Each day, Mike and I packed a lunch, picked up his buddy, and went to different beaches. I relaxed and read while the two boys ran on the sandy beaches or splashed in the water. On the phone, Chris asked me, "Can you get Becky back home in time for the birth?" It hurt that she wanted her sister, but not me. I replied, "Nothing short of a miracle could make that happen."

Later I called her declaring, "The miracle has happened." My children know that God has always worked miracles for me, so no one was surprised. This is how the miracle took place: on those days on the beach with Michael, not only was I praying and thinking, but I was also reading the help wanted ads in a newspaper. One available position intrigued me, even though I did not meet the qualifications requested. So on our way to the beach the following day, we stopped to inquire about the position of counselor in a summer camp for emotionally disturbed teens. The camp administrator asked me more and more questions. Then, to my surprise, he said, "We pay fifty dollars per day. You work four days on, two days off. You will get room and board for you and your son, and lake privileges for both. When can you start?"

Two hundred and fifty dollars a week! It was amazing! The Lord sure works fast!

Rebecca's airfare was eight hundred and fifty dollars, and only a day prior it might as well have been eight thousand five hundred for all the chance I had of raising it. Not only did I get the job, but money was advanced to me for the plane ticket.

I started working the next day...and loved it. The children there had often suffered abuse at home, both emotionally and physically. Confrontation techniques were used, and I learned that even a short fifty-year-old lady like me could accomplish a Brownsdale hold. Some children just needed a human straightjacket to embrace them when they became violent. As they screamed accusations and insults, we responded to everything they said with honest, clear answers. I found that these young people would eventually share the deepest emotions or questions in their hearts as we subdued and then comforted them, so long as we were sensitive to what they were saying.

"I hate your guts!" they would scream.

A counselor responded, "There are times when I don't like myself either."

"I hate all women!" another one might yell.

Response, "We're not so bad when you get to know us."

"Why did my mother start raping me? I was four. Why? *Why?*"

"I don't know why," the counselor would say, "but it was wrong. I'm so sorry this happened to you."

After counseling there all summer, Family Advocacy helped me put a down payment on a house...which I paid back. I was given charge over five disturbed teenagers while also teaching school again in the fall. Now my little house was full. All five went to public schools, and we all arrived at my home around the same time.

A sixteen-year-old Mexican boy, small for his age, stands out. When he was angry with me one time, he yanked the phone from the wall and hung it high in a tree in the backyard.

If I sent him to his second-story bedroom, he would jump out the window, rolling into a ball as he landed so he wouldn't get hurt. When he seemed to be missing in the morning, I would sometimes find him sleeping in a tiny cupboard where he felt safe.

There was insignificant Pat, large in body but timid in spirit. What could we give her for her fifteenth birthday to make her feel loved and cared for? I prepared a beautiful birthday cake, and at ten minutes past midnight, everyone in the house trailed into her bedroom, singing "Happy Birthday to you!" Her eyes opened wide as we circled her bed, but just as she started to sit up, I tripped, with candles, cake, and all. My aim was tragically good—it smashed in her face, and we stared in stunned silence. Then we burst out in laughter. It was certainly a birthday to remember!

Michael was so fascinated by all that was taking place in our home. When I went to my first PTA meeting at his school, all eyes were on me. Michael had repeated daily all the wild tales of what was happening at home with those he referred to as his brothers and sisters. Everyone thought he was making up the stories—who would believe that Luke would insist on standing in the yard to pee, or that Ralph would moon people when angry, or that his Mexican brother—a Mexican brother!—would sleep in a cupboard? There was much explaining on my part, but really, there are some things that cannot be explained.

* * * * *

Mike and I were in for a special treat when Sri Dhyana joined our family. She was barely a year old. I vividly remember the night of her arrival. Rebecca had convinced Bob to go with her to the airport and pick up the little traveler, who had been put on a plane in Chicago. Looking like a miniature glamour girl in her diaper, sandals, and sundress, Sri toddled around from room to room, ignoring me completely. Rebecca and Bob took

134

off right away, as it was late and Bob had no desire to stay for long.

So there we were! By one in the morning, my eyes could stay open no longer. The fire in the fireplace made the room cozy as I stretched out on my back, sinking into the soft carpet. After another quick tour of the house, this little creature with her exotic name straddled my chest, inspected my closed eyelids, then lay her tiny head on my shoulder. I was in love. When Mike arose in the morning, he was ecstatic with the little nymph.

Right away, she was his princess, and she wrapped him tightly around her little finger—a bond never to be broken, despite the nine years of age between them. From the time she arrived, this little girl was a free spirit. Life for her was and is one big adventure, to be fully enjoyed.

There would come one late night in Maine, several years hence, when warm hurricane winds were blowing, making trees bow low, that I paused from my work of freelance proofreading to look out the picture window and enjoy the night's wild beauty. My imagination seemed to play tricks on me as I saw a small apparition floating on the lawn. As it didn't disappear, I went out to investigate.

There was three-year-old Sri, in a long, white, frilly nightgown, whirling and twirling in the strong wind at one in the morning. I could not believe she had slipped right by me to dance in the storm and let the wind carry her wherever it chose.

When I first learned of Sri's coming arrival, I felt as if I could identify just a bit with a country song that was popular, which went a little like this: "This time, Lord, you gave me a mountain, a mountain that I cannot climb." As it was, Mike and I were barely surviving. At age ten, Michael had taken a paper route, and his money was often used to feed us. How could I stretch our money more, hire a babysitter, and buy more food while maintaining the teaching career that sustained us? How was I to know that what was so hard for me then, were to be two of the greatest blessings in my life: Sri and Michael.

* * * * *

Because of the added expenses, I sought added employment. I found it in teaching adult education, and it was like hearing from on high the words of Isaiah 30:21: "This is the way, walk ye in it." I loved teaching day school, and I enjoyed teaching night classes.

I was a depression baby, brought up in the back woods of Maine, and then moved on to the jungles of Brazil where I completely missed out on what was happening in the world from 1950 until well after 1970. Our infrequent trips to the United States were spent mostly traveling and not participating in the culture of the era. There was so much right here in the United States that I knew nothing about, but God introduced me to Cynthia Tanous and Joe Pease, who became like mentors as they helped me catch up to the times.

What started out as a job teaching adults to read expanded into teaching English classes and GED classes in the evening. It bothered me to leave Sri and Mike alone for hours at a time, but a solution came when my car broke down completely and I bought a Toyota Dolphin recreation vehicle—it was like a miniature home on wheels. I could leave them in there to eat, sleep, read, or play games. One summer, I parked in the schoolyard as students came into the motor home to be tutored, while Sri played out on the swings and slides and Mike rode his bike and kept a watchful eye on his princess.

Sri and Mike grew very close, so when Sri's mother came to get her after a few years, Mike was inconsolable. His heart was broken; Sri felt the same way. When a few months later, Sri returned to our home, I knew they would be afraid to freely love and unite as a family, fearing from experience that separation could come again with no warning. Indeed, their fear of separation from each other and from me was strong. It was at this point that I went to a lawyer I knew I couldn't afford, but also knew was necessary.

Once Sri's adoption became final, the stress level went down, and ours became a happy, relaxed home again. Meanwhile, adult education went forward. Here there were no visible snakes or serpents to defeat, but I felt that my work was just as important as the work God had given me in Brazil—I was in a different world, with different people, but always with the same God. Cynthia Tanous, my adult education director, recognized in my missionary background that I was less traditional and unafraid to try new things…so she sort of turned me loose to teach where and how I saw the need, as well as for a few classes and individual students she set up.

This brought many new experiences for me, including teaching students in their homes when they couldn't come to class. Life was wonderful—I had two beautiful children at home (or in school with me as I taught evenings), and all the people I could squeeze in time-wise to teach. Wow!

A few stories about the people I taught truly show my excitement about teaching. In one trailer home, the mother of five small tykes needed desperately to get away from an abusive husband. When I taught her, neighbors would drop by and join in the lesson. I always had three to five extra students. They all worked hard at lessons, which made it fun.

The mother felt that, if she could get her driver's license, she could get a job and leave her desperate situation. One day I really had to go to the bathroom. I went into her bathroom and not only was the toilet clogged, but people had filled up the tub with pee and poop. The stench was putrid. These were the conditions the woman was trying to escape from, which made it a pleasure to help her.

Soon I was teaching five nights a week and all day Saturday. When Cynthia asked me to tutor a pregnant teenager who wanted to graduate with her class, there were no hours left… unless you considered six to eight in the morning. To my surprise, everyone agreed to this. I would get Sri and Mike out of bed, then put them in my motor home where they would go

back to sleep and wait for the alarm clock to go off at seven—
just in time to eat breakfast and get ready for school. Arriving
at the student's home, I would go in the house that had been
left unlocked by the dad on his way out to work. Usually, this
meant getting her out of bed and to the breakfast table. As she
ate, I taught and corrected papers from the day before. She was
groggy and very pregnant, but she always had a good attitude
and spent time during the day on her studies.

Another student, whom we'll call Sandra, was quiet and shy
but eager to learn and glad to be back in school. As our English
classes progressed, we became better acquainted, and I learned
of how God had taken her only son just a short time before, at
the age of nine. He had been allowed to ride in the back of his
father's pickup truck, along with a five-gallon can of gasoline.
When the truck veered off the road, only the dad came out alive.
Sandra felt grief and anger, not only for the death of her only
child, but also because she felt her husband had been careless.
Through the years, I have noticed that a child's death in a family
will either bring parents closer together than they have ever
been, or split them wide apart.

The latter had happened there, but circumstances were
holding things together…for the moment. Sandra was a soft
person, whose main goal in life had been to be a good wife to her
husband, upon whom she was completely dependent…and who
she felt, in a way, had betrayed their family with the accident.

Her husband Skip was a macho person and just couldn't
imagine that this live blonde doll he had taken care of for over
ten years, and acted as if he owned, wanted to leave him. In a
desperate act to keep her, Skip paid a visit to a psychiatrist who
agreed that some treatment might be a help…for Sandra. And
that Augusta State Mental Hospital could be the place to do it.
After all, any woman who would entertain thoughts of leaving
such a wonderful man as Skip, along with the new house he had
built for her, must be insane.

We missed Sandra in English class; the other students told

me that she was quite ill. It was rather a surprise, then, when she showed up one day with her husband in tow. They both sat through class, but it was a struggle to read Sandra's eyes. Finally, when it was break time, she followed me to the bathroom, and with tears in her eyes, told me she was not only being held against her will, but she was also kept doped up. She was not crazy, and she begged me to help her make an escape.

Somehow she had convinced Skip that she needed to attend class and pick up her English assignments or she would be in trouble. Now she depended on me to know how to do the rest. Many thoughts raced through my mind. I could call the police, but whose side would they take? Sneaking her out was out of the question; there was no back door to the upstairs bathroom we were in, and it led directly to the teacher's room. Then thoughts of my little aborigine girl Eva, the one I rescued from two warring mothers, came to mind. My technique had worked once…so why not again?

Standing in front of Skip, I prayed for boldness and a lack of fear. He listened as I explained that I strongly felt Sandra needed a change and should be where she could be calm, quiet, and alone, to think things out, and I felt that she should come spend a few days with me. I had but one thought—to get her away from Augusta. Skip questioned me for a while and then agreed to the plan. It was God's will that swayed him, certainly, and maybe also respect for a teacher's judgment that won him over.

From the moment we got into the car together, Sandra relaxed completely. She felt safe and loved and had someone to help her. Soon we found a decent regular job for her so that she could survive on her own. Next came the divorce and, all in good time, a new marriage, which has proven true down through the years.

* * * * *

Each of my students mattered; some left deep impressions,

however fleeting our acquaintance—like teenaged Holli, struggling to make a place in this world for herself and her small son.

Holli

When I met her, I knew she was neither child nor adult.
The world was her enemy; people existed to insult.
Looking deep in her eyes I instantly knew
Trusts had been broken, those she loved, been untrue.
Thank you, Lord, for letting me help a little.

- Betty Williams

* * * * *

Another student, whom I'll call Amy, had long blonde hair that came down to the middle of her back; her petiteness added to her doll-like appearance. Both she and her husband were in my English class and were good students. When summer came, Amy needed one more course to graduate, so she came to my home to be tutored. I tried every trick I knew to grab her interest but just couldn't do it. Finally, I suggested she write an autobiography starting at age fourteen. This way, I could correct her grammar and explain grammar rules; and when she rewrote her story, learning would take place.

It certainly did for me, though I don't know about her. Through her writing, I learned that she attended my class at gunpoint—actually at gunpoint—from her husband. She had been a prisoner at school as well as in her parents' home and then her own home. When she found courage to run from him, he took all of her belongings and made a big bonfire in the yard with them. How could I have been so insensitive to her needs? Amy graduated from high school and went on to a better and more fulfilling life.

Both inspiringly and sadly, there were so many students like her.

Tammy was one—a soft-looking, sandy-haired girl in her late teens. She had so much potential that even when she was high, her gift for writing shone through. This was a gift God had given her, and the best I could do was to draw it out from her. Tammy and I bonded, but she wanted more one-on-one time with me, more attention. She tried to accomplish this one evening by slitting her wrists. When I arrived early to teach the eighteen students in my English class, she showed me her bloody mess. I asked her how long ago she had done it, and learned that it had been an hour before. I thought, *well, if she hasn't died by now, she most likely isn't going to.*

I gave her clean rags and told her to keep them around the wounds and that we would take care of them after class. The following day, Cynthia Tanous found a way to fulfill Tammy's emotional needs—in part—by arranging for Tammy to be a voluntary aide in my fourth-grade classroom. At the end of the first day, Tammy presented me with a beautiful poem she had written. When I finished reading it, she asked if I liked it.

It was amazing writing.

Then with an evil grin on her face, Tammy picked the poem up, held it high, and tore it into a thousand tiny pieces. There was no humor in her act, though. After tearing it, she threw it in the wastebasket and ran laughing out the door.

I sat stunned for a few minutes and then remembered how many hours it had taken Tammy to make me a large Christmas wreath out of small, round red and white peppermint candies. Now I would return the favor and take a few hours to glue the poem, one tiny piece at a time, back together.

After class the next day, I said, "Tammy, I want to read something to you." It is a shame there was not a camera rolling to record her expression as I slowly read every word of her poem.

Tammy graduated from college magna cum laude. Today she is out there making her mark on the world.

George was a truck driver. On his way home from work one night, he stopped for a cool drink. When a man touched him close to where he kept his money belt, his response was automatic; both men ended up in the hospital—George with a broken fist, and the other man with a broken jaw. But in the classroom, none of his violent side came out. Learning to read was a priority for him. If a student canceled a private lesson, I called George, and he would drop whatever he was doing to race over to the classroom. What a joy he was to teach! One night he showed up to class with a freshly boiled lobster for me—the sweetest one I had ever eaten.

A call came for me to tutor a handsome young man of sixteen in a school outside of my regular district. The teaching area was a space with a small desk and two chairs under the basement stairway. The only other person present was a wandering janitor, so it felt a bit spooky. After teaching Jimmy for a few weeks in this eerie setting, we settled into a friendly routine. One day he left for the bathroom and came back sort of sullen. He sat in the chair beside me and opened the flaps of his unzipped pants, exposing himself completely—leaving nothing to the imagination. It was unexpected and really unthinkable that this teenager should make a pass at a woman so much older than he was.

I took a few seconds to decide how to react. There were things to consider. Number one, the janitor was out of earshot, and number two, so far he was just offering and not insisting. So I completely ignored his behavior and continued teaching. Somewhere along the line, he discreetly put it all back in and zipped it up tight. He probably felt there was no harm in asking.

I decided not to share the incident with anyone after looking at the simple facts: it would be his word against mine, make a nasty stink, and he could always use the excuse that his exposure was an innocent act. Needless to say, I learned some valuable lessons through this experience. Teaching, especially one-on-one, should always be done in a clearly visible area, preferably with more people present than just a single student. I decided not to return to that school unless the environment could be changed.

* * * * *

I have always said that being acknowledged or appreciated for hard work and effort did not matter, as long as I could feel God's hand on my shoulder and hear him say, "Go for it." But then I received a letter that meant a lot to me. It read:

Mrs. Williams,

> When I called in mid-December to obtain information regarding your evening classes, I had been praying to God for days to provide the best GED opportunity for my son Todd. After my initial conversation with you, God gave me peace, and I knew that Todd would be in good hands. After these past six weeks, Todd has continued to express his enthusiasm for your evening classes; and he always acknowledges his appreciation of your teaching style, compassionate care for your students, and your sense of humor.
>
> Isaiah 30:20-21 says "And though the Lord give you the bread of adversity, and the water of affliction, yet shall not thy teachers be removed into a corner any more, but thine eyes shall see thy teachers. And thine ears shall hear a word behind thee, saying, this is the way, walk ye in it, when ye turn to the right hand and when ye turn to the left."
>
> For Todd's life, you are the teacher he has eyes upon. God has changed Todd's life and provided Todd with renewed hope. Thank

you for being a blessing in the life of many
students, including Todd!

Sincerely,
Dave Stallard

I felt pretty good about that.

* * * * *

One of the stories I read to my children was about a small
bunny that became so hungry he ate a whole garden of lettuce.
The farmer was amazed at this feat and praised him highly. The
bunny could not understand why, because he was only doing
what came naturally according to the dictates of his heart. I felt
a kindred spirit with this bunny when I was presented with a
"Teacher of the Year" award in adult education. I enjoyed every
bit of what they did for me—a fancy presentation and trip to
Montreal with everything paid for, including a babysitter. But I
had just been doing what came naturally.

It was strange. I had been teaching an older Frenchman and
his daughter for years. Each year, when the two of them went to
Montreal, he wanted to take me, my children, and his daughter
to go see the maple syrup flow through troughs and get boiled
down to syrup; he wanted us to eat their special baked beans,
hear the live bands play, and join in the celebration. When I
finally went, I participated in all that he had talked about…but
he had passed away three months earlier. Sometimes life works
out that way.

* * * * *

Now I was busier than ever, both in teaching and at home
with the kids. Mike and Sri were loaded with energy. Mike used
his in swimming at the YMCA, playing baseball, rollerblading,
bike riding, and playing a drum in a drum and bugle corps. Sri

started gymnastics and was also a majorette, twirling a little baton. Gymnastics turned to dance, and little did we realize that it would become a large part of her life—she went on to tap, jazz, and ballet dancing over the years. Christmas for us involved her performances in nineteen productions of the Nutcracker Suite, starting out as Marzipan and moving up to representing a flower and a snowflake. We spent many days at the Maine State Ballet Company, supporting her. I joined in the costume-making crew to utilize my time while waiting for the seven hours of dancing to end on Saturdays.

It was always good to be involved in my children's lives.

Chapter XV

And One More is Three

$\mathcal{T}$he voice on the other end of the line was urgent. "Mom, this man just can't handle it anymore. He is turning his seven-year-old son over to the state. Mom, they are already putting the label 'emotionally disturbed' on the kid. Think of what will happen to him if he is passed from foster home to foster home! He won't survive! Mom…he is a nice little boy." Chris was really concerned for the child.

My head was swimming. Could I help another young one? Should I do it? Mike, Sri, and I were making it, but just barely. I decided to talk it over with Sri and Michael. I told them about the call.

"I don't know if he is black, white, or Chinese," I told them. "And I don't care right now, because if we make a decision based of the color of his skin, it is the wrong decision."

Neither child hesitated.

"I'll share you, Mamae, and all my things," Sri said. For her, this was a big deal—she hated sharing me with anyone, even Michael and Rebecca.

Mike told me I could use the paper route money he had been saving for a trip to Niagara Falls to go get the child. Our family gave a green light, so I called the boy's father.

He seemed relieved to have a home in which to put the boy, instead of giving him to the state. We chose a spot on the map halfway between Maryland and Maine where we would meet—Danbury, Connecticut.

My children were ready to move over for one more, but fellow workers and relatives thought I had flipped. I actually felt guilty and ashamed to tell anyone I was adopting another son, because I knew it met with such disapproval. Still, how can a person say no to another human being? Isn't this what life is for?

"God," I prayed, "Don't place me in these positions without giving me the strength and wisdom to fulfill them."

Thankfully, my sister backed me up one hundred percent. I was working, so I had little time to make the trip and needed to drive straight through. She wanted to go with me so I wouldn't be driving all night alone. Her husband didn't want her to go; he said, "I've prayed about this, and I just know God is going to take care of Betty."

She replied to that, saying, "I'm glad! Now I'm sure He will take care of us both! My sister really needs me and I know you'll understand." Not only did he understand, but he took care of Sri that day and showed her such a beautiful time that she continues to remember it as a high point in her life.

We arrived at the rendezvous. There was a Puerto Rican man with two beautiful little boys who were as opposite from each other as anyone could be. David, the seven-year-old, had shiny golden curls all over his head; his four-year-old brother had black shiny curls all over his. After quick introductions, we sat and had a bite to eat. Then, David was given to us. He clung to a brown paper bag, which contained a few clean clothes. We later learned that David didn't know what was going to happen to him until he was on his way to meet us; then he was given a hand-written note signed by his father saying I had custody over him. What a frightful experience for any child!

We were tired. The rain came down in torrents, but there he was on the back seat, a frightened golden child in our car. We felt at peace with God and each other.

This little guy was something else. He seemed to be at one with animals, but Heaven help a human who got in his way! If he played baseball and struck out, he'd chase the other kids with the bat and swing to hurt. Two days after he arrived, Sri had her fifth birthday. We had a party at McDonald's with a few friends and relatives. David was like a lion let out of a cage. He ran from table to table, snatched food off plates when he could, popped every balloon he could find, thoroughly enjoying the sound of both the pop of the balloon and its owner yelling at him. I couldn't wait for the party to end!

Adults had polite smiles plastered on their faces. My uncle Winnie kept assuring me that the lion could be tamed and encouraging me to have patience. I couldn't hold David because he would scream and holler...but nor could I let him go on pushing kids and insulting adults—he had a wide repertoire of vulgar insults. My faith wavered. Perhaps love, kindness and all those good things were not really enough, I feared. Worst of all, Michael and Sri were enjoying every one of David's words and actions—he dared to do things they had never even thought of. "Lord, what did *You* get me into?" I prayed.

When we all talked at night, I would say to the child, "Don't take your anger out on the three of us. Remember, we are the good guys." Oh, how many times that happened...

With one more mouth to feed, I had to consider money ahead of personal desires. With this in mind, I started teaching English evenings from six until ten at night at Elan, a residential high school in Poland, Maine. By then I had two full-time teaching jobs and threw in a few adult education students on the weekend. I also picked up work freelance editing for a printing company and would do that late at night while the kids were sleeping. I worked hard, but I loved and enjoyed the little family I supported.

Then once again my apple cart was overturned—sometimes life seems like a big lesson in attachment and impermanence. Our beloved principal left, and the new one did not like me from day one. He would pop in on me many times, trying to catch me in a vulnerable moment. This didn't work, so he did little petty things to make me look bad, increasing his power over me and, he thought, decreasing my desire to work there anymore. Sometimes when the children went out for recess, he would end it early, telling the other teachers but not letting me know—I was teaching fourth grade that year in a mobile room not attached to the main building, so I didn't get the intercom messages.

Then he would march my students to my room, blaming me for not being outside to greet them. He picked up on things I said, misconstruing my meaning and sometimes even implying that I meant something obscene by them; he had never heard the quaint phrase "received his due share" and accused me of saying "he received his douche."

A child brought in a book of fairy tales for me to read aloud, but as I started to read, the stories didn't seem appropriate for the age level. He called me in and asked about it, then tried to imply…well, I wasn't sure what exactly he was trying to imply, and it became terribly awkward for both of us. I finally insisted on having another person in the room during his verbal attacks, which infuriated him even more.

This all attacked my nerves; and for the first time in my life, I had an ugly thing called shingles. My face was quite broken out and red. I knew I must move on, so I quickly sold the small trailer we had been living in, called in sick to school, and went to a friend's small cabin on a lake where I could get stress-free and calm down…and pray about my next move. I kept the three children with me, which made relaxing much easier. Mr. Man thought perhaps I was faking my illness and, with a few other people, went to my humble abode to make an unexpected visit. Imagine his surprise when not only was I not at home, but also my home was not at home—the mobile had been hauled away! He was the one who got the surprise, standing there looking like a buffoon.

August 27, 1995

I am bleeding—deep down internal bleeding
That wells up colorless and pours down
From the eyes.

Hate, derision, and separation are mine.
They arrived in an isolation package—
A reward for years of love and sacrifice.
If these gifts are poured over me—will I recognize?
Ah yes. Many years have passed
But the pain is a familiar one.

- Betty Williams

Chapter XVI

A Teacher Reborn

*W*hile in refuge, I applied to Waldoboro and Rockland for a new position. I was offered interviews at each of them…on the same day. Waldoboro hired me on the spot and wanted me to return to pick up the contract. There was not time to cancel Rockland's interview, so I kept it; and they also wanted to hire me! At last I felt good about myself again. Two schools really wanted me—my hope was reborn. Yes!

A board member in Rockland called my house and encouraged Mike to help me decide to go there. The new position even offered four thousand more a year than I was making! My shingles went away. I walked with confidence but didn't formally retire my old position until August. A worker in the office confirmed that the principal had been trying to bully me into leaving and was going after a sixth-grade teacher next. I called that teacher in the summer and warned him, but he didn't believe it. Four months later, he called to ask me where I had received my information, which of course I couldn't share, and confirmed that it was true after all. I felt so lucky to be free.

So there we were, the four of us beginning what became ten more years of being in a wonderful place to live and work. I called the adult education center director, Tim Dresser, who gave me a corner in his teaching program so that I could work more hours and reach more students. How God takes care of us! I continued to do what I loved, to teach in a stress free environment, and to enjoy raising my three children. When problems inevitably came along, we rose to deal with them with gratitude for all that still remained right.

* * * * *

Sri Dhyana enrolled in a small Christian school, where they invented a rule that if a child earns less than an eighty-five grade point average the parent must attend the school for a day. I went before this little group of men (God forbid, it felt, that a woman should be found in a leadership position such as the head of the household) after hours one day, fully intending to withdraw my child before submitting to their demand. Accusing eyes were on me as I was told again and again what a bad mother I was—not willing to sacrifice one day's pay for the good of my child. That day's pay would make a difference in paying bills, of course; I could have withstood their judgment, but I didn't, and gave in. I was truly disappointed in myself that I actually allowed myself, at my age and after all I had gone through, to be punished and humiliated by being forced to take off work and follow my daughter around through her classes for all to see—the very example of a failed parent, it implied.

I felt attacked and dumped on spiritually as I sat in Sri's school and listened to the teacher's steady drone; I couldn't hear what was being said, but it was clear that a power struggle was over, and I had lost.

There was a highlight, though—my Sri shone like a diamond, hugging me, doing little things for me, so happy to have me there with her at school. A friend asked her, "Doesn't it make you nervous to have your mother here?" She answered, "Oh no. We're best friends; she's not just my mother." She was my silver lining to that day's dark cloud.

The situation was wrong all around—I was wrong to submit, and they were wrong to humiliate me. I don't believe God's name was glorified in any way.

I Am Strong, You Know

I am strong, you know,
Tried by experts,
Left lonely on bare floors
And hated by those who loved me.
Nights of sadness have not taken away my life,
Nor days of melancholy and madness.
I am a quiet cave hidden in ocean rocks,
A fir tree watching giant redwoods rot away,
A patch of grass at the edge of a roaring river,
A stone that has known the desert's heat
And survived till the sun was gone.

I am strong, you know,
Oppressed by tyrants,
Abandoned on dark nights
And cursed by those who praised me.
Winter's raging has not bowed my head,
Nor years of loneliness and aging.
I am silent spring trickling down the mountain,
A patch of snow refusing to melt,
A patient crack in granite rocks
A tree that was bent at birth
But has not fallen in the cold wind.

I am strong, you know,
Some kind of woman has somehow grown.
I like the strength that lovers give,
But I am strong enough alone.

- **James Kavanaugh**
  © 1977

Chapter XVII

A New Start

*M*ike was going on to college in the fall; the house we rented was seasonal, and coming up on the summer when the owners would return to it, we were homeless. Why not have a summer to remember, we thought? I took my summer's pay in a lump cash sum, and the four of us divided it into four envelopes. One was for gas and other car expenses, one was for food and sleeping accommodations, one was for entertainment, and the fourth was for emergencies. I placed four tall rectangular plastic containers upright in the trunk of the car. Each person filled theirs with anything they wanted, including clothes, books, and personal belongings.

The day after school closed, we headed out. Mike was in the driver's seat, I was the navigator beside him, and Sri and David were in the backseat—which caused constant arguments until Michael came up with a bright idea. Each time the two in the back seat argued, they were to sit five minutes quietly with an arm around the other's neck. David hated this, but Sri thought it was great—making the punishment that much more effective— and it made the trip much more peaceful.

We were to go anywhere we wanted to go. Our first stop was Chicago. We visited museums and walked on the beach of Lake Michigan. Then we carried on west and camped in Yellowstone National Park, where the buffalos roamed around our tent at night, and Old Faithful shot up like a fountain each day. Mike took control of putting up the tent and cooking, so for me it was a true vacation. Then we visited the Grand Canyon, the Painted Desert, recreations of the London Bridge and Aztec ruins, the Winchester Mansion in San Jose, California, Chinatown in San Francisco, and giant redwood trees in Mendocino, California… among other places pretty exotic to Mainers.

Then we visited my sister Jean's house, where she and her husband Bob welcomed us. Sri celebrated her ninth birthday there, and the rest of us dragged out the presents we had been hiding for the occasion. It proved the last time we saw Jean alive, and I was always glad we made the trip if only for that reason.

We made fewer stops on our trip back; it had taken us a month to get to California, but only two weeks to go home. We packed in quite a bit during our six-week vacation. I can still feel the delight Mike had when driving near the Pacific Ocean around hairpin curves on a road with a drop of over a hundred feet and no guardrails. Driving fast so close to the edge was one way to age very quickly...or not.

Years passed in a blink. David graduated from high school at seventeen and signed up for a five-year stint in the Navy. Sri was close behind in age, and similar in her ambitions to see the world. The summer before she graduated, she went to Brazil with a teenage missionary team from New Tribes Mission and was amazed to be placed with two good friends Bob and I had worked with so many years before—Ed and Maggie Harper. It truly is a small world.

Time has a way of continuing on, no matter what is happening in one's life. Time uses its power to heal; time uses its power to make people forget; time closes the door on one chapter in life and opens another.

* * * * *

Sri, eager to graduate from high school, earned her diploma at sixteen and entered college in the fall. As is the way with the young, she fell in love the following year and was married a few days before her eighteenth birthday. At the ceremony, Sri was right in her element with the ocean breeze making her satin wedding gown gently swirl around her legs. As the tide came in, the sound of the waves surrounded us; and the bridal couple stood with the deep blue of the ocean and its whitecaps in the background—quite the picture.

It was the best family reunion in years. Christina came with all her children and grandchildren around her; she looked stylish and much younger than her years. Becky came, beaming with pride at the little family she was trying to hold together. She looked old-fashioned and sweet in her little cotton dresses, and the heirloom diamonds on her finger and ears just sparkled.

Mike was there on leave from the Navy, wanting to take over running the reunion for me but was not quite sure how; he felt that peculiar pain of Sri becoming married and thus even more grown up, but did not share much about it. Almost everyone was there, and the few who weren't, were missed—and missed us. That's the way our family is, and the way we shared that peculiar feeling of Sri leaving us—of growing up—as she left the altar a married woman.

Spending time with my granddaughters, I saw so much of my life reflected in them—hopes and questions, struggles and uncertainty, and brash courage. It was heartbreaking and funny at the same time, and justified, if just a little, what I had seen and felt in my life. Kysha had a painful childhood which she determined to put behind her so that she could confidently be herself; I related to her unfinished dreams and the painful ambiguity, where one moment her mate seemed wonderful and in the next she was ready to flee all the way to Alaska to get away. Sonya sent the message to the world "I'm making it, and I'm going right to the top! I'm beautiful, inside and out!" And she is; her confidence inspires me.

Lena reminded me that life is never over, so long as you are alive. She devoted herself to her babies and husband, and also to herself, as if her mission in life is to raise them all for God. Sharla, nineteen years old at Sri's wedding, has the courage to speak out for truth—that kind of energy that comes from being young and full of ideas in that beautiful time of life.

After the wedding was over, my life felt empty. The echoes of David, Sri, and Michael were all around, though they were out in the world making their own places; memories of our times together poured over me. After one year of emptiness, I told myself, "I am not dead yet, and I am not going to live on memories, no matter how wonderful they are! I am getting out and making new memories!"

I retired from all three of my concurrent teaching jobs, sold my home, bought a Chevy conversion van, and took off for a visit with my sister in Alaska. I had made that 5,500-mile trip years earlier with Bob and vowed that I would make it again, though this time alone. Once again I was trying to make a statement that with God's help, the seemingly impossible can be done—like a grandmother driving alone to Alaska! Don't ever be afraid to live while you are still breathing.

It was a worthwhile 11,000-mile round trip; time spent with those you love is never wasted.

Retirement is just not for some people. I missed teaching. So, from Alaska I went directly to Baltimore to teach first grade in a Christian School, where I enjoyed a snug apartment after some people at school discovered that I was living in my van— they objected to that, and took care of me. Mike was close by in college, and we spent some very good time together. Sri also joined us, attending the same college and teaching dance— though displaced from Maine, I was home wherever my family gathered.

*****

I became like a wandering minstrel, going whichever way the wind was blowing, living life to the fullest and always teaching. In Georgia, while visiting Rebecca and her family, I taught seventh grade special education. That required a special teaching certificate, which I had rather incidentally picked up before, and it became something of a passport to teaching opportunities.

I also taught in inner city Baltimore…and loved it. My teaching tour of anti-retirement took me back homewards

160

to Lewiston and Kittery in Maine and then back to Seward, Alaska.

I even went back to Brazil, where friends came from all corners of that country to spend time with me. Those who were teenagers when I left mission work were by then adults with families of their own. Wanda, who had leapt over that cobra in her path on our walk so long ago, had become a fearless teacher and raised six boys—three of her own and three nephews—and her hopelessly outnumbered daughter. Wanda's husband had been ill for more than ten years when I visited. He was paralyzed from the waist down and bedridden, but she had cared for him, feeding, bathing, and grooming him daily with the help of her family. I was amazed to find in her kitchen cupboard the dishes, obviously cherished, that I had given to her when I left Brazil.

She mothered me all during my stay. With the help of her daughter Daisy and son Lincoln, her family bought me a gold ring that has remained on my finger since the day they put it there—I was adopted into their family, as I had adopted Wanda into mine so many years ago.

Becky's childhood friend Socorro was the same as ever—still the baby of her family. A man named Hugo and I became close friends; and after I left, he decided to accept my invitation and come to the States; he sold his motorcycle to pay his fare and arrived in Boston. He lived with me for a year, learning English and working for Michael. Then he went out on his own to discover what our United States is all about.

My homecoming in Brazil was a flurry of old friends and new, as I caught up with the lives of so many people who were dear to me in my missionary days. Valnoisa, a neighbor girl from the village of Tocantinia, was all grown up and owned two homes; she welcomed me into one of them, inviting Soccorro as well. And there was Concita, who witnessed Wanda jumping over the cobra so long ago and had learned to play the piano while listening to Becky practicing each day; Concita's skill at the piano was a source of well-earned pride.

161

Then down from the north came my little aborigine girl Eva, whose rescue inspired me to liberate Sandra from her abusive husband; oh, how Eva and I hugged and cried. She had traveled a whole day on a bus to reach me, even though she was just getting over dengue fever. Her long jet-black hair hung down to the middle of her back, and she looked the same as ever in spite of the hard life she had lived. It was like a dream come true. I doubt Mother Teresa ever got a nicer reception than I did on my visit back to Brazil. After boarding the plane back to the States, a cord around my heart broke, and I cried uncontrollably for half an hour while the steward stood by helplessly.

A year later, news reached me that my sister's partner was dying. Her two grown sons no longer lived at home; and having just gone through it myself, I knew how traumatic living alone for the first time in your life could be. Now was the time for her to cash in on my promise that if she ever needed me, I would be there. She needed me, and so I went back to Alaska—gladly. Being needed outweighed my fear of unnecessary flying.

To be homesick for a place without its people anymore seems strange to me; but after ten months, I had quite the yearning to get back to Maine. Alaska had been good to me; and when my legs gave out completely, it was God's grace that brought my sister Sistie to help me. The doctors there were wonderful, and I got a clear message from an acupuncturist when he looked me dead in the eye and said, "You have a bad case of homesickness and need to leave…right away." Returning to Sistie's house, I called the technical school where I had picked up work and started packing to leave. Knowing how much I hated flying, my sister decided to drive me more than five thousand miles back to Maine.

Now that is true love.

In Canada, we saw the vivid colors in the sky of the aurora borealis. We saw the gigantic folded mountains and many deep blue lakes. It was wonderful to be going home.

Once back in Maine, my pains and aches all disappeared; and the next two years were virtually pain free…so imagine my surprise when a routine checkup found a three and a half by seven inch lump in my stomach. I needed an immediate operation, and a surgeon came in to see me. He tried to calm me by saying how many such operations he had performed, what number in line my operation would be, and that if his knife slipped and cut into my bowel it would not really be his fault… and that having a colostomy for the rest of my life would not be so bad, since many people learn to live with them.

Nothing about that reassured me. To me, I am a person; to him, I was a number, like a cow in a slaughterhouse being looked over for the best place to cut off a steak.

Then it was my turn to ask questions. "Are you a heavy drinker?" I asked. "No," he said. "Why?" "Well I don't want you to get drunk over the weekend and operate on me on Monday," I said. Then I asked what type of music he plays while he operates. He just stared at me when hearing this question; but his nurse, with a big smile, told me exactly what his poor taste in "operating music" was.

When I walked out of that office, I was determined that no doctor who considered my belly as number 563 and saw me as an obstacle between him and a golf course would come near me with a knife.

Articles in magazines all say to get a second opinion. With this in mind, I drove to Laconia, New Hampshire. I assumed all Maine doctors would back each other up, but a physician in a different state would care less.

If I were to be operated on, the New Hampshire doctor was the man I wanted to do it. He took a personal interest in me right away. But, when he took my x-rays to a board of doctors, they determined my lump was on an ovary and not on the intestine as previously thought. It was then that I learned that each surgeon had a right to slit only one part of my body; if something goes beyond an imaginary line, it is another doctor's territory. No longer would the man who welcomed me so graciously do the operating, unfortunately—it was in another doctor's territory.

There is an expression that goes "When in doubt, don't." I was surely in doubt, so I didn't. My stomach had been cut open six times previously, leaving a deep indentation and a field of scars; I didn't want any more surgeries than necessary…or truly, any at all.   So then it was just between God and me. Having been favorably exposed to alternative medicine in Alaska, I turned to God and alternative medicine. The D'Adamo Clinic in New Hampshire embraced me. They did many things to rid me of toxins, but one of my favorites was mud. It came in slabs they put in an oven to heat. Then I stretched out on top of a large piece of hot mud, and small slabs were placed on top of me before my being wrapped like a pig in a blanket. I never perspired like that in all my life! It felt so good. They had me change to a sugarless, high-protein diet and take up Tai Chi. I did it all.

When they left me alone for half an hour with acupuncture needles in me, I prayed, "God, please remove this lump in my tummy." When soaking in a tub with special minerals in the water, I prayed again for the same.

The end of a long day's treatment was rewarded with a massage using a special lotion—magical, no doubt. My body dropped away, and I was left floating on a cloud. From the cloud I decided that if the lump killed me, I was going to die happy.

So far, I haven't died…and I'm still happy.

* * * * *

Leaving Maine for treatment in Baltimore was a hard decision, but God had someone there ready to take over. When Dr. Stark first came at me with an acupuncture needle, it looked as though he was aiming for the top of my head. I put my hands

164

up to shield myself and yelled, "Not my head! Anywhere but my head! You can't be going to stick a needle in my head!" Gently moving my hand, he responded, "What? You mean here?" So there I was, with a needle sticking out of my head. And I was fine.

His office featured a hyperbaric oxygen chamber. I had heard of one in Alaska, but had never been in one. Propaganda had it that cancer cells could not live under pressurized oxygen. If that were true, and the thing in my tummy was cancerous, it might be a good way to stop its growth. I had nothing to lose— but money—and a lot to gain.

To me, a chamber meant a room, but not in this case. I found what looked like a plastic coffin with windows in it. I bravely climbed in, demanding a small brown paper bag in case I hyperventilated—you know, a bag from which to breathe in oxygen, within an oxygen chamber. Doctor Stark did not laugh at my ignorance as he handed me a bag. Things were going pretty well until I glanced over at the doctor as I got into the chamber, which I told myself was less like a coffin and more like a tiny little spaceship. He had a handful of acupuncture needles, and the first one was aimed right at the top of my head again.

I spent most of my forty-five minutes inside the chamber holding my stomach and praying, "Dear God, please remove this lump from my tummy."

After six months, an x-ray showed the lump was two-thirds of its original size, and so it continued shrinking until it was gone. I am not sure how God continues to use old people, but I am sure he still has work for me.

* * * * *

If cats have nine lives, then I'm like a cat with eight of them gone; I'm well into my ninth for sure. My first life found me crying alone at night in the children's home; then I went to Bible school in Rhode Island where I met Bob and had yet another life when I got married and had my first baby in Chicago; another life began in California during missionary training; and another in South America with my husband and seven-month-old daughter; then I spent another life in Maine after returning to finish college at the age of fifty; I had another when I taught in public and private schools for twenty-five years; and another when I retired and drove alone the ten thousand miles to Alaska.

While writing this book, I reflected on the many kind people who have mattered in my life—people like Corrine Palmer, Cynthia Tanous, and many others. When I first started out, I could never have imagined all that God had in store for me. I am truly blessed, many times over.

Johnny Appleseed wandered far and wide, spreading apple seeds as he went. I, too, traveled far and wide, spreading seeds to help spirits and minds grow in places from Maine to Georgia and Alaska to Brazil. God has packed so much into my one small life, and who could ask for anything more?

One of the nicest gifts God gave me was a tickle-button that allowed me to see the humor in many situations. I am sure God has a sense of humor and gave a pinch of it to me, and that has made all the difference.

All the way, my Savior leads me, what I have to ask beside?
Can I doubt His tender mercy, that through life has been
my guide?

-- Fanny J Crosby

Selected Poems by Betty Williams

Growing Old

Each day my vitamins I take
To keep me big and strong, to
Help me to remember things and
Pray nothing will go wrong.
Still my belly sags, my wrinkles
Deeper grow. My hair is a little
Grayer and my reaction a little
Slow. But deep down inside
Of me, my heart is just the
same.

I cling to the love of Jesus,
Ever calling on His name.
The hurts of younger years,
Have long since passed away,
I trust in God completely to
Guide me through each day.
Most pain that I feel now, is
Towards those for whom I care,
Going through so many trials, I
Can only help by prayer.

On Being Old

They are sitting on benches outside of the mall, heads bowed with the shame of having grown old.

People passing by, looking but not seeing the pain of unfulfilled dreams—a life gone by, a story untold.

~ or ~

She jumps as the car nearly hits her, surprised at the lack of concern.
She smiles as a finger is lifted; she knows they have much to learn.

~ or ~

In the hot car she snoozes and waits for the family shopping to be complete.
She's glad they took the time to include her so she waits with her memories, again to repeat.

Untitled

Death is coming my way
I am not afraid
Death is coming my way
I wait in silence.
I do not scream out
I do not fight against it
I do not anticipate
I simply accept it.

Important Dates in Betty's Life

Born: July 21, 1927, in Auburn, Maine
Named after: Mumma's sister, Betty Elaine Pray, who
               died at age 14

- 1945 Graduated from high school at age 17
- 1948 Married Robert McMillian Williams,
        September 11
- 1949 Christina born in Chicago on October 21
- 1949 Left for Brazil on New Tribes Mission plane
- 1951 Elizabeth born and died on September 13 in
        Cochabamba Brazil
- 1952 Rebecca Gail born in Anapolis, Brazil on
        December 31
- 1953 Returned to States for series of operations on
        Rebecca
- 1956 Returned to Brazil
- 1962 Furlough in the States
- 1963 Returned to Brazil
- 1969 Back to the States
- 1972 Adopted Michael at age 3—he was born August
        31, 1969
- 1972 Returned with Becky to Brazil for a visit
- 1976 Graduated from college at age 48
- 1976 Started teaching in Turner, Maine, public school
- 1976 Divorced Bob
- 1979 Adopted Sri Dhyana, age 1—she was born July 15
- 1985 David joined our family at age 7
- 1987 Left Turner, Maine, to teach in Rockland, Maine
- 1996 Retired from public schools
- 1996 Drove to Alaska and back in a conversion van at
        age 69
- 1997 Taught in Baltimore

- 1999 Returned for visit to Brazil
- 2000s Taught in:
    -- Georgia
    -- Maine
    -- New Hampshire
    -- Alaska
    -- Baltimore, MD

Select Letters From Brazil

Written largely by Bob, and documenting the family's adventures

October 14, 1957

Dear Friends,

Today is Sunday, October 14, 1957, in Belem (Bethlehem), Para, and all the senses—of sight, of hearing and feeling, of taste and smell—eloquently and harmoniously confirm the fact that we have finally reached the shores of Brazil once again. It is now over three years and four months since we left Belem for the States to have little Rebecca cared for. Such a long time, it seems, but we look back upon these years and months as a time of further preparation. A time of renewing old acquaintanceships, and also a time during which we have become acquainted with many of you for the first time. We are truly grateful to God for the great encouragement you have been to us, and thankful as well for those who will be sharing in our labors, striving with us through your prayers.

We finally left New York the evening of September 21 aboard the British Motor Ship "Velaz" (Fast), which might have been more correctly named "Vagaroso" (Slow), arriving in Barranquilla, Colombia, exactly one week later. While there we visited some Presbyterian missionaries who told us about the persecution of Protestants in Colombia under the direction of the Roman Catholic Hierarchy. Since 1948 when it systematically began, 75 Protestant men, women, and children have been butchered because of their faith of Christ. 47 Protestant church buildings have been destroyed by fire or dynamite, many others damaged. More than 200 Protestant primary schools have been closed. (Only 50% of adults are literate) Since January this year, more than 40 Protestant churches have been closed. These figures are documented. How many others have suffered is not known. Pray for Colombia.

We left Barranquilla on Monday, October 1, arriving in Trinidad the following Friday. The first two weeks went pretty well as the sea was not too rough, sailing through the islands and into the Caribbean Sea. Only the first few days out of New York were uncomfortable, as the children had not yet acquired their sea-legs. But when we left Trinidad Friday night, heading out around the Gianas, and began to buck the Gulf Stream, the little ship began to rock and roll violently. Each day we looked for it to calm down, but for 6 days and nights we were tossed about without let up 'til we entered the Amazon. The children made out very well, for which we were very thankful, hardly missing a meal. Betty had the worst time of all. She went to bed the night we left Trinidad and stayed there until we arrived here a week later. She ate very little and could keep down nothing of what she did eat. Daddy managed to put in an appearance at the dining room at least once a day, and, with the exception of one breakfast, was able to keep things down by going right to bed, where he also spent most of the last week. We were reminded many times of the Scripture verse above.

How glad we were to awake Friday, October 12, just 3 weeks from the day we left New York, and find ourselves at anchor in the Amazon River a short distance from Belem. When the launch came out to bring us ashore, how happy we were to see Roger and Ellen Bailey on board to welcome us back and help us through customs.

At daybreak this morning we were abruptly awakened by the sharp reports of fireworks, which seemed to come from all quarters, gradually reaching a crescendo. As the Brazilian waiter aboard ship had hoped, we had arrived in time for the "Festal de Nazare," (Feast or Celebration of the Consecration to the Virgin of Nazareth). This celebration will go on for two weeks, beginning this morning with a procession, and ending up with a similar one two weeks from today.

After breakfast, as I sat here in the sala (living room) looking out over the neighborhood, I suddenly became aware that the noise of the fireworks had gradually given place to beautiful choir music, floating in on the fresh, fragrant, morning air from some neighbor's radio. A gentle breeze, which bordered very near to being cool, was swaying the neighboring palm trees. Every now and then one of the legions of big black buzzards (South American garbage disposal agents) ruffled his feathers and flew to a more advantageous perch to wait for some discarded morsel. With their bald heads and long black plumage, they are often referred to as the Friars.

Presently we were reminded again of the Festal, of which we wanted to take pictures so folks at home might have a better understanding of the idolatry of this people. Inquiring of Sinval, a Brazilian lad who helps out here at the receiving home, we learned that the procession had already begun. Sinval offered to accompany people; the bus could go no further. Leaving the bus we began to press our way through the waves of people. The first few blocks we moved right along, being carried along with the current. We drew near the Praca da Virgem (Place of the Virgin). We had to squeeze through inch by inch.

People were everywhere, crowding every window and balcony, on roofs, even perched in the trees. Realizing we would have to get above the crowds to take any pictures, we scanned the area for a vantage point. Surprised that no one had as yet taken over such a find, we made a beeline toward it. By the time we reached it, a lad had climbed up on the posts but consented to share his post with me. Nearby stood the massive cathedral, and all around as far as we could see, a great sea of humanity.

As the procession arrived, and the image of the Virgin was taken from the carriage, the multitude began to clap their hands and cheer, and as many as were near thronged in after it. Afterwards the crowd began to recede as the people returned to their eating and drinking, gambling, and merrymaking. One could not help but be reminded of the words of the Lord in Matt. 9, where Jesus, looking on the multitudes, was moved with compassion, because they were scattered abroad, as sheep having no shepherd—"The harvest truly is plenteous, but the laborers are few; Pray ye therefore the Lord of the harvest, that he will send forth laborers into his harvest."

Sincerely in the love of Christ,
New Tribes Mission   Bob Williams
                    Missiao Novas Tribus
Woodworth, Wisconsin
Vianopolis, Goias
                                                                    C a i x a

Postal 7

December 25, 1957

"Go ye therefore, and disciple people of all nations…"

Dear Friends,

Season's Greetings from Brazil. As we come to the end of another year, we find ourselves again taking inventory of the year's activity. This year…we made our first trip to the Xerentes Indians during May and June. In September we left Vignopolis, moving up here as a family to Pedro Alfonso to carry on the work with Xerentos, arriving here October 8. Also during October we made our first visit to the Grao Tribe. And then in November we were again able to visit the Xerento village of Baiza Funda, which has all kept us on the "go," but as to the "making disciples" we find more difficult to calculate. We have had many opportunities for preaching and have witnessed professions of faith in Christ. But as we look back over the year, there are few, it seems, of whom it might be said that we were instrumental to a great degree in their becoming Disciples of Christ. Looking back we find that this year has not passed without failure and loss, but we also feel that this can by no means be compared with victory and blessing which has been ours this year.

As we had hoped at the time of our first letter, Glen and I have been able to return to the Xeronto village of Baixa Funda to begin the work again where we left off last June. Just before leaving Pedro Alfonso, we were told by some Indians passing through town here on their way to visit another village,that everyone at Baixa Funda was down sick with the flu, and that three had already died. The next day we were on our way up river by boat to Tocantinia, about 75 miles to the south. There we were able to obtain medicines from a government dispensary, but had to wait there a whole week for animals to make the 45-

mile trip in the village. By the time we arrived, most everyone had recovered, but we were saddened as we were told of Vito's passing away while the others were helpless to care for him. He was one of the few who professed to believe in the Lord, but we could only hope that he really knew what it meant to put his trust in Christ. For the others was the sober realization that their day of opportunity was eternally gone.

The food situation of the Indians was rather lean this time. Because of rumors that the S.P.I. (Indian Protection Service) was going to move them all away to another area, many were discouraged, having sold all their rice, their staple food, and were planning to leave the village. So there was little variety in the menu which mainly consisted of macacheira, a sort of potato-like root, cooked into a thick, starchy, stringy gruel, and farinha, which is made by grating and toasting a noxious cousin of the macacheira family after the poisonous juice has been extracted, which resembles and tastes something like fine gravel. Occasionally, there was fruit or a bit of wild meat.

The Indians were all busy cleaning and planting their fields, so we were not able to accomplish as much teaching as we had hoped. Not being able to have organized classes, we endeavored to take advantage of their idle moments to teach them individually. Some are beginning to read quite well. We also taught the better readers some simple arithmetic. Evangelistic meetings were not well attended, conferring the spiritual ministry also to an individual basis. We sought first to find out how much they had remembered from previous visits. Many remembered the songs and were often heard singing or whistling the tunes as they went about their work. As to their ability to grasp and retain spiritual truths, it seems as if Satan has washed away the good seed as they remembered very little of what they were taught. We realized anew the shortcomings of the trade language in trying to reach their darkened hearts with the Word of God in terms they can comprehend and appreciate. Our effort was renewed in obtaining more Xoronto words and phrases, which should help in the analyzing and utilization of the data already at our disposal. We were also able to get the poles up for a school building, which the Indians agreed to finish by the time we again returned.

The night before we left Baixa Funda, we met with the chief and a few others to ask them if they really understood our purpose in coming to them, and as to their attitude toward us and the message we came to bring them. Well, they expressed many doubts as to why we wanted to help them, as in the past years other missionaries and anthropologists had visited them, speaking of helping them but had not returned. They just couldn't understand why it was that we had left our people and the comforts of the "Cristdo" (Christian, loosely—civilized) to spend our time with them, and as to what it was we were trying to tell them they were quite confused. So once again we started at the beginning and told them about God's making the world and that he so loved the world that Jesus, His Son, left all of Heaven's glory to come into this world of sin, sickness, and death, to die for the sins of the Xerento as well as for the Cristdo, and that He might give peace, joy, and eternal life to all who would simply believe in Him. Only God knows their hearts, but for us it was the highlight of our visit with them, as their attitude toward us seemed much warmer than at the first. They expressed their desire that we might return soon, promising the school building to be done.

As we look back upon the work among the Xerentes, it seems as one of the real setbacks has been that the missionary has only been able to spend a week or two at a time in the village with long intervals, sometimes several months, in between. This has been partly due to the continual change of personnel due to sickness and the shortage of workers and partly because of the difficulty of transportation. We wonder how much further along the work might be if someone were able to be with the Indians more consistently without the lengthy intervals.

Our problem right now is the lack of transportation. In

October, in order to spend two days with the Craoo, we traveled over ten days; and in order to spend ten days with the Xerentes in November, we were gone three weeks. We have considered buying animals, but good ones are expensive; and we have no place to keep them, neither here in town nor at the villages, nor do we feel we can spend the time to take care of them properly. We also considered the possibility of a pair of lightweight motorcycles, but they would take quite a beating because of the mud, water, and sandy places (covering) over ten miles at a stretch. A jeep with 4-wheel drive would surely solve the transportation problem. We would be able to arrive the same day, ready to go to work instead of feeling well spent. Then, too, we would not be limited as to the amount of supplies. But we are confident that the Lord will supply that which is needed for transportation, and we would appreciate prayer on this behalf. We are laying aside as God prospers for this purpose, and any who wish to participate are welcome to do so.

But pray especially for a harvest of souls among the Xerentes in '58. Pray also as we cooperate with the Baptist church here in Pedro Alfonso as they have not had a pastor for some time, and so we have this added opportunity as we are home with the family here in town. Pray also for Betty as she conducts children's classes, and for the desire of my heart to provide something that will be a blessing to the young people here, especially the older boys. Pray especially this coming year that God would grant us to see among the Indians as well as the town folk, not just professors of religion, but real Disciples of Christ.

Sincerely in the love of Christ,

Bob and Betty Williams

New Tribes Mission
Missao Novas Tribus
Woodworth, Wisconsin   Pedro Alfonso, Goias, Brazil

April 4, 1958

"For we wrestle not against flesh and blood…"

Dear Friends,

It's hot and sticky. Myriads of gnats are buzzing around, attempting to make life miserable. As I sit here in my hammock, swatting and scratching, I think.

I think of many of you who have not heard from us for some time now and are wondering how the work among the Xerentes is coming along. Occasionally, my thoughts are brought back here to Baixa Funda by the noisy chatter of the Indians across the room, loudly engaged in conversation. From others, seated at crudely hewn benches nearby, comes an undertone of ba-be-bi-bo-bu's as they painfully read from their syllable charts or primers, laughing heartily at times at one another's boo-boo's.

Komoamani looks over my shoulder as I write. He picks up one of your letters and asks, "What's this?" I yell at him what a letter is and how it came from a friend far, far away by a plane like the one pictured on the postage stamp. I shout, pointing to the sky, "Like the one that flies over your village every week on its way over Brazil." He laughs stupidly and drifts away—he is quite hard of hearing.

Samoru watches me scribbling away and innocently asks, "Are you writing?" Of course. I say, "Yes," politely, as I say to myself, "Whatever did you think I was doing?"

Then I wonder as Wakuke tells me that he knew I was coming. The night before I arrived, he dreamed several times that he saw Tiago, a nearby farmer, coming toward the village, leading his pack mule, accompanied by a taller red man. I was red all right, like a lobster. Got a terrific sunburn on the first day I left Pedro Alfonso.

I wonder also, as I consider these people and their attitude toward the Gospel, if you folks at home get the same picture of them from our letters as we see of them here. If you could meet them individually and work with them, surely your hearts would be concerned.

Wakuke, who goes by the Portuguese name of Florenco, is undoubtedly the chief of this village, though he does not boast to be. He is old but works harder than all the others, who for the most part have an aversion to work. He is friendly and cooperative and studies so hard at his syllable chart, but seems to get nowhere. He speaks Portuguese crudely, but fluently, and has no difficulty expressing himself. His son Wazakru, (Rondon), however, is one of the best readers, though very spoiled.

Then there is Dbara (Jose) and Dabuzurkua (Bernaldo) who have professed to believe in the Lord over a year ago. The more intimately we are able to talk with them, the more we wonder if they have not been baptized prematurely, as they are not even good professors, not to mention the lack of any accompanying fruits of salvation.

There is Samaniu (Firmino) and Samoru (Luis) and Sakrubi (Joao Paulino) and Slinikru (Joao Calixto) and the many others who, it seems, understand Portuguese quite well. But as you look deeply into their eyes and endeavor to reach their hearts with God's message, they shrug their shoulders with indifference and declare that they do not know what you are talking about.

Sincerely in the love of Christ,

Bob Williams
New Tribes Mission
Missao Novas Tribus
Woodworth, Wisconsin   Pedro Alfonso, Goias, Brazil

About the Author

Muma, Can You Hear Me? is Betty Williams' retelling of her favorite stories, as though a monologue to her mother. It is her first book. Betty wrote the manuscript during her youngest daughter's deployment to Iraq with the Maine Army National Guard, as a way of connecting with both her mother and her daughter through the power of storytelling.

Born in Auburn Maine on July 21, 1927, Betty Elaine Williams was raised by a single mom during the Great Depression. She married in her 20's and joined her husband in missionary service in Brazil for twenty years.

Always capable of teaching those around her, she developed that gift into a thriving professional life. She taught thousands of students both young and old, in Brazil and across America. Her family changed with her divorce, then grew again when she adopted three more children as a later-life, single mother with a teaching career.

Betty once again resides in Auburn, Maine. Thanks to her youngest daughter, she texts on her cellular phone, has a Facebook account, and still loves a good game of Scrabble.

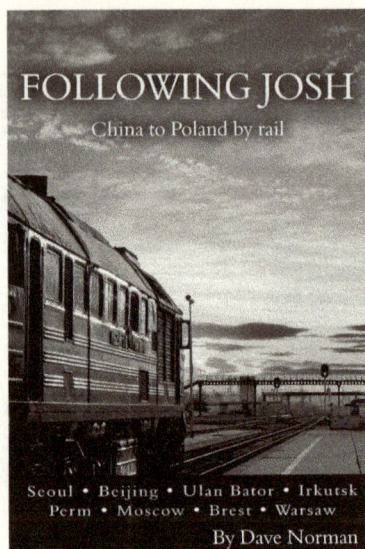

Also from f/64 Publishing

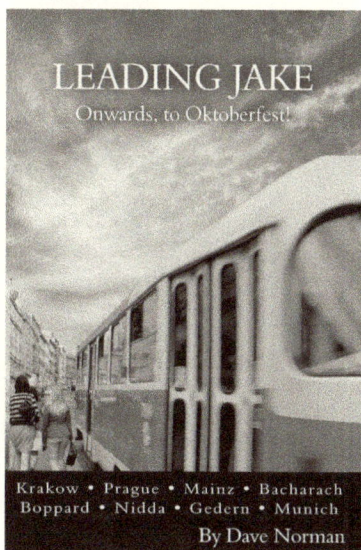

LEADING JAKE
Onwards, to Oktoberfest!

Krakow • Prague • Mainz • Bacharach
Boppard • Nidda • Gedern • Munich

By Dave Norman

Available Now!

The adventure begun by author Dave Norman in his acclaimed travelogue **Following Josh** continues in **Leading Jake**, where Dave meets his best friend in Krakow — a medieval city with an ancient soul and a youthful lust for life. Their coming-of-age story is set against rich historic and cultural backdrops as they explore Krakow and Prague. Then alone at last in Germany, land of his ancestors, Dave must make peace with former loves and other trauma before embracing a new life.

From absinthe bars to Auschwitz, a fire-breathing dragon's lair to Oktoberfest — and that space between extended adolescence and adulthood — **Leading Jake** is the provocative, laugh-out-loud sequel to **Following Josh** that will inspire you to fall in love with life...and laugh with every breath.

www.leadingjake.com

www.ingramcontent.com/pod-product-compliance
Lightning Source LLC
LaVergne TN
LVHW011229080426
835509LV00005B/402